# THE ROMAN WORLD SERIES

GENERAL EDITOR: F. KINCHIN SMITH, M.A.
*Senior Lecturer in Classics,*
*University of London Institute of Education*

## PLINY

Selections from the Letters
Edited by C. E. Robinson

## CATULLUS

Selections from the Poems
Edited by F. Kinchin Smith and T. W. Melluish

## VERGIL

Selections from the Eclogues, Georgics and Aeneid
Edited by W. F. Jackson Knight

## SELECTIONS FROM LATIN PROSE
## AND POETRY

An Anthology, edited by
F. Kinchin Smith and Barbara Hodge

*Opinions*
*on the Series expressed by Senior Classics*
*Masters and Mistresses*

'. . . wholly admirable, interesting, cheap and full of the social background which most texts so sadly lack."—*Grammar School*

"I consider the edition of Pliny a good one. ... the Catullus possibly the most admirable edition of a classical author for schools that I have seen."—*Public School*

"I am most impressed."—*Girls' High School*

"They are the most attractive editions that I know."—*University Professor*

"A delightful book; pleasant to hold and read."—GREECE AND ROME

"Wholly delightful."—JOURNAL OF EDUCATION

# CATULLUS

# CATULLUS

*Selections from the Poems*

(together with translations of three poems by F. L. Lucas)

EDITED BY

## F. KINCHIN SMITH, M.A.

SOMETIME SCHOLAR OF TRINITY COLLEGE OXFORD, SENIOR LECTURER
IN CLASSICS, UNIVERSITY OF LONDON INSTITUTE OF EDUCATION

AND

## T. W. MELLUISH, M.A.

SOMETIME SCHOLAR OF CHRIST'S COLLEGE, CAMBRIDGE
SENIOR CLASSICAL MASTER OF BEC SCHOOL

LONDON
GEORGE ALLEN & UNWIN LTD
MUSEUM STREET

FIRST PUBLISHED 1942
REVISED SECOND EDITION 1946
FIRST IMPRESSION 1947
SECOND IMPRESSION 1948
THIRD IMPRESSION 1950
FOURTH IMPRESSION 1952
FIFTH IMPRESSION 1953
SIXTH IMPRESSION 1956
SEVENTH IMPRESSION 1958
NINTH IMPRESSION 1966
TENTH IMPRESSION 1969
ELEVENTH IMPRESSION 1971



ISBN 0 04 874001 2

REPRODUCED AND PRINTED IN GREAT BRITAIN BY
REDWOOD PRESS LIMITED, TROWBRIDGE & LONDON

# GENERAL INTRODUCTION

Twenty-five pages of Caesar or Cicero, and five hundred lines of Ovid or Vergil, are a poor return for four years of Latin, yet this is all that most of the 30,000[1] or so boys and girls in England and Wales, who annually take the School Certificate, read of Latin literature. If they continued their studies further and read some Catullus, Lucretius or Tacitus, this meagre pre-School-Certificate diet might be excusable, but less than 10 per cent. continue the study of Latin beyond that examination. It is as if we taught a French boy English for four years and gave him nothing to read except twenty-five pages of Wellington's dispatches or of a speech of Burke, and five hundred lines of *Paradise Lost*. No Shakespeare, Keats or Tennyson—no plays or lyric poetry. The idea of the Roman World Series is to give these 30,000 pupils first-hand acquaintance with more of the great literature of Rome before they ' drop ' Latin for ever.

The time has come for a different orientation in the teaching of Latin. The aim of Latin teaching should be the understanding and appreciation of Latin literature. Reading must be wider and more intelligent. There must be more study of what the Romans did and felt and said when they were not fighting. ' The great pagan civilisations march their eternal round ', said the late Sir Walter Raleigh, ' like weary ghosts through the schoolroom ; at the stroke of the clock they vanish, and the activities of real life are resumed. Hardly does the thought occur that these too, like other restless spirits, have a message to deliver, and are burning to speak.' That there are Roman writers besides Caesar, Cicero and Ovid, burning to speak, and intelligible with the right help to the young, is the belief behind this series.

The first three volumes consist of selections from Pliny's letters and the poetry of Catullus and Vergil. It is hoped to produce further volumes on the same lines, of authors chosen for the interest of their subject-matter to the modern world. As Mr. C. E. Robinson says in his introduction to the first volume of this series, ' the Modern World is nearer to the Ancient World than

---

[1] e.g. 29,386 offered Latin in 1945.

to the period which lies between.' From answers to a questionnaire sent recently to certain schools, it was found that Pliny was the least read of Latin authors, but when read the most popular. His letters deal with a period of Roman history that is more interesting and important to us to-day than any other. His style, if more sophisticated, is less involved than Caesar's, and difficulties will diminish through the interest of what he has to say.

The second volume introduces a poet who was as human as Burns, as unashamed in love as Donne, and as frank as modern poets in expressing what he felt and thought. At present Catullus is rarely read before the School Certificate examination, but when a boy or girl does make acquaintance with ' the tenderest of Roman poets nineteen hundred years ago ' it may be an experience that will last a lifetime. Much of Catullus is harder than Ovid, but some is easier, and most is more interesting.

The third volume is *Vergil for Pleasure*, by W. F. Jackson Knight. Vergil, according to Christopher Hollis, is ' one of the very small company whom it is necessary to understand if one is going to understand anything.' This is planned as a book to be read straight through by those who sincerely wish to share, with millions of their predecessors, the wonder of Vergil's ' ocean-roll of rhythm ', and the wisdom which ' human grandeur's most exalted voice ' can impart. The book is arranged as a continuous story built on passages from Vergil himself (his *Eclogues* and *Georgics* as well as the *Æneid*) and the English poetry he has inspired. The book contains much which will be new even to those who know their Vergil well ; the fruits of the most recent research and of many years devoted to the study of Vergil.

In the text of these volumes difficulties are reduced where necessary by omissions, but not by alteration of the original words. In the belief that knowledge of background should be acquired through the reading of authors themselves, rather than from ' cram ' books on antiquities, the text is interwoven with English commentary on relevant aspects of Roman life, history and literature. The notes, printed at the bottom of the page to assist rapid reading in class, stress the cultural not less than the linguistic side. Explanations of syntactical points are left mainly to the teacher.

F. KINCHIN SMITH

# CONTENTS

(The traditional numbers of the poems are given in Roman numerals)

# CONTENTS

# ILLUSTRATIONS

# PREFACE

IN this selection an attempt has been made to choose those poems or portions of poems of Catullus which are the easiest and the most suitable for reading in the third and fourth years of Latin. To facilitate rapid reading in the short time usually allowed in schools, help has often been given in the notes at the foot of the page which some teachers might prefer to supply themselves, but many grammatical and syntactical points have been left for the teacher.

We have attempted to arrange the poems in a more logical order than in the usual texts. The traditional order, which seems purely a metrical arrangement (the first section lyrics, the second long poems and the third elegiacs), is so irrational and so detrimental to the appreciation of Catullus as a poet, that no apology is made for this. To read in the eleventh poem of Catullus's final repudiation of Lesbia and to come upon the first expression of his love in the fifty-first poem, is the height of absurdity. Imagine reading straight through a selection of Keats or Shelley arranged by metres.

No attempt has been made to perform the impossible task of an accurate chronological arrangement, but the Lesbia poems have been arranged and interspersed through the book in three sections, the sections corresponding to the course of Catullus's love affair. The poems have therefore been given new numbers, but the traditional numbers have been added (in brackets) in Roman numerals.

The Introduction on ' Catullus and English Poetry ' is an attempt to provide suggestions for those, whether pupils or teachers, who may like to contrast or compare some personal poetry in the two languages.

In preparing this edition we gratefully acknowledge considerable indebtedness to Ellis's *Commentary*, and to Munro, Macnaghten and others.

We wish to thank Mr. G. M. Young, Director of the British School at Athens, for the photograph facing page 36, Mrs. Flecker and Messrs. Martin Secker & Warburg for permission to include James Elroy Flecker's translation of Catullus' 'Phaselus Ille' from the Collected Poems of James Elroy Flecker, and Major the Hon. Maurice Baring and Messrs. W. Heinemann Ltd., for permission to include the translation of 'Siqua Recordanti' from *Have You Anything to Declare*.

## PREFACE TO SECOND EDITION

WE have taken the opportunity of a new edition to include the parody of 'The Old Yacht' (Phaselus Ille), usually attributed to Vergil, which is not easily accessible, and to correct a few minor misprints.

*September* 1946

# INTRODUCTION

Catullus and English Literature

In comparison with the influence that Latin writers such as Vergil, Ovid and Horace have had on English poets, it is surprising that that of Catullus has not been greater. That his poems were known in Rome during the century or so that followed his death we know from the many complimentary references to him in Martial. Pliny read him, and Horace owed him a debt, although he does not acknowledge it. Horace followed the revolutionary idea of Catullus of adapting Greek lyric metres to Latin, and in at least two poems the direct influence of Catullus is almost certain. In his conversational piece with Lydia (Odes III, 9) there is an echo of the *Acme and Septimius*, and the Sapphic poem *Integer vitae* suggests in other phrases besides *dulce ridentem* the conscious imitation of his predecessor; but the light-hearted playfulness of Horace has little in common with the passion of Catullus.

In the five hundred years after Martial, Catullus is occasionally quoted by writers, and tantalising references are made to poems which we no longer possess. In the Middle Ages he was forgotten; nor should we expect his poems to have been read in the monasteries. They were lost for centuries until a scholar of Verona, Catullus's own birthplace, found one day at the beginning of the fourteenth century an ancient manuscript hidden under a bushel measure. This single manuscript disappeared again afterwards, but not before copies of it were made, and the two great Renaissance scholars, Petrarch and Boccaccio, had a chance of knowing Catullus well. Of these copies, one is in the

Vatican and the other at Oxford. Chaucer, who borrowed so freely from Ovid and Vergil, seems not to have known Catullus, but Skelton almost certainly did, as we see from *The Nun's Lament for Philip Sparrow*. This was written shortly after 1500, and laments the death of a bird killed by a cat in an Elegy of more than thirteen hundred lines!

> When I remember'd again
> How my Philip was slain,
> I wept and I wailed,
> The tears down hailed;
> But nothing it avail'd
> To call Philip again
> Whom Gib our cat hath slain.
>
> . . . . . . .
>
> It had a velvet cap,
> And would sit on my lap,
> And seek after small worms,
> And sometimes white bread crumbs;
> And many times and oft
> Within my breast soft
> It would lie and rest.

That Catullus should have made a special appeal to the Elizabethan love poets was to be expected. Recollections occur in Wyatt, who brought to English poetry the inspiration he had found in Italy, and in Sir Philip Sidney. Sidney translates poem 32 to illustrate the inconstancy of woman.

> 'Unto nobody', my woman saith, 'she had rather a wife be
> Than to myself; not though Jove grew a suitor of hers.'
> These be her words, but a woman's words to a love that is eager,
> In wind or water's streame do require to be writ.

The influence of Catullus on English poetry is most marked in the Marriage Hymns so popular in the Elizabethan

age.   Spenser's *Epithalamium* is full of the spirit of the
Marriage Song (poem 29), which Catullus wrote to cele-
brate the wedding of his friend Manlius to Aurunculeia.
The ' boyes ' running

                              up and downe the street
          Crying aloud with strong confused noyce,
          As if it were one voyce.
          Hymen, io Hymen, Hymen, they do shout ;

the bride coming forth

                              with portly pace,
          Like Phoebe, from her chamber of the East,

          .   .   .   .   .   .   .   .   .   .   .   .

          Her long loose yellow locks lyke golden wyre,

and the description of the end of the day, when ' the bright
evening-star with golden creast ' appears out of the East
and the bride is brought ' into the brydall boures ', all recall
Catullus.
   In the two lines

          Open the temple gates unto my love,
          Open them wide that she may enter in,

the five words of Catullus live again :

          Claustra pandite januae :
          virgo adest.

Ben Jonson, who studied the Roman poets when he should
have been laying bricks, inserts into his play *The Barriers*
an actual translation of the beautiful simile in Catullus's
other Wedding Hymn (poem 24, ll. 39-58) :

   Look how a flower that close in closes grows,
   Hid from rude cattle, bruised with no plows,
   Which the air doth stroke, sun strengthen, showers shoot
          higher,
   It many youths, and many maids desire ;

The same, when cropt by cruel hand 'tis wither'd,
No youths at all, no maidens have desired.

.    .    .    .    .    .    .    .    .    .

Virgins, O virgins, to sweet Hymen yield,
For as a lone vine, in a naked field,
Never extols her branches, never bears
Ripe grapes, but with a headlong heaviness wears
Her tender body, and her highest sprout
Is quickly levell'd with her fading root ;
By whom no husbandman, no youths will dwell ;
But if by fortune, she be married well
To the elm her husband, many husbandmen
And many youths inhabit her then.

Ben Jonson also adapted the famous *Vivamus, mea Lesbia* (poem 15), which has also been translated by many other English poets, including Crashaw and Coleridge.

Difficult as it is to solve the riddle of Shakespeare's sonnets, no one who has read them can doubt that Shakespeare went through an experience similar to Catullus's, which he expressed in even greater poetry concerned with a rival who betrayed him and a Dark Lady, beautiful and nobly born, but false to her marriage-vows and false to her lover.  The course of passion is traced from ecstasy and love, through doubt and jealousy, to disillusionment and hate.  Poetry is not biography, and what matters to us is not the historical details of the experience, but the sincerity, directness and beauty of the poems in which the experience is expressed.

In Sonnet XVIII Shakespeare says :

Shall I compare thee to a summer's day?
Thou art more lovely and more temperate :

but by the time he reaches Sonnet CXLVII, he writes :

For I have sworn thee fair, and thought thee bright,
Who art as black as hell, as dark as night.

It is improbable that Shakespeare ever read a line of Catullus, but the language of the deepest feelings of the heart is the same in London as in Rome, and it is not surprising to find the infinite regret for a past love expressed in the same terms by both poets.

> Cum desiderio veteres renovamus amores
>     atque olim missas flemus amicitias.
>
> (Poem 10)

> Then can I drown an eye, unus'd to flow,
> For precious friends hid in death's dateless night,
> And weep afresh love's long since cancell'd woe,
> And moan the expense of many a vanish'd sight.
> (Sonnet XXX)

The poets of the seventeenth century also were influenced by the spirit of Catullus, especially Herrick and to some extent Cowley. Herrick's lyrics, epigrams and especially Marriage Hymns reveal his debt to the Roman poet. He acknowledges this in the toast :

> Then this immensive cup of aromatic wine,
> Catullus, I quaff up to that terse muse of thine.

In the lines *To Anthea*,

> Give me a kiss, and to that kiss a score :
> Then to that twenty add a hundred more :
> A thousand to that hundred : so kiss on,
> To make the thousand up a million.
> Treble that million, and when that is done
> Let's kiss afresh, as when we first begun

there is an obvious imitation of the *Vivamus* lyric, the more successful because of its brevity. It would be easy to collect line after line that shows similarities, if not actual borrowings. But Herrick's ' conceits ' and affectation are utterly foreign to Catullus, and he is incapable of the Roman poet's passionate intensity. A poet who only 'plays around the heartstrings' is as far removed from the sincerity and depth of feeling of Catullus as Horace is from Shelley. Donne, who as a young man loved and hated with the same intensity, would have had much in common with Catullus.

> For God's sake hold your tongue and let me love

might be described as the most Catullan line in English poetry.

In the eighteenth century, when poetry sprang from the wits rather than the heart, the influence of Catullus was naturally less. Pope took the idea, though little else, of the *Rape of the Lock* from Catullus's translation of Callimachus's *Lock of Berenice*. He could not have gone to the original Greek, since it is only some fifteen years ago that fragments of the poem were found in the sands of Egypt. He did not, however, translate any of Catullus's poems.

Swift made many versions from Horace, but only one, it seems, from Catullus, which deserves quoting, as it captures something of the terseness of the original quatrain (poem 30):

> Lesbia forever on me rails.
> To talk of me she never fails.
> Now, hang me, but for all her art,
> I find that I have gained her heart.
> My proof is this : I plainly see
> The case is just the same with me ;
> I curse her every hour sincerely,
> Yet, hang me, but I love her dearly.

The common-sense of the Augustan age was unlikely to be sympathetic to a poet who 'loved, not wisely, but too well'. There was one poet, however, in the eighteenth century who, although it is unlikely that he ever read a word of Catullus, has more in common with him than has any other modern poet. Burns possessed the same tenderness, humour, sensuousness, and sympathy with man and nature. In both poets we find the same coarseness without depravity coupled with a simplicity and sincerity which hated sham and baseness.

> My love is like a red, red rose,
> That's newly sprung in June

is nearer to Catullus than most translations.

It is natural that two poets of such similar natures should express themselves alike. ' The language of nature ', said Gibbon, ' as also of love, is the same in Cappadocia as in Britain,' and many of Burns's lyrics such as *Ae fond kiss* and *When I think of the Happy Days* could be matched by poems of Catullus.

Perhaps the most successful translation of any poem of Catullus is a version of Poem 14, done into the dialect of the Scottish poet by G. S. Davies :

> Weep, weep, ye Loves and Cupids all,
> And ilka Man o' decent feelin' :
> My lassie's lost her wee, wee bird,
> And that's a loss, ye'll ken, past healin'.
>
> The lassie lo'ed him like her een :
> The darling wee thing lo'ed the ither,
> And knew and nestled to her breast,
> As ony bairnie to her mither.
>
> Her bosom was his dear, dear haunt—
> So dear, he cared na lang to leave it ;
> He'd nae but gang his ain sma' jaunt,
> And flutter piping back bereavit.
>
> The wee thing's gane the shadowy road
> That's never travelled back by ony :
> Out on ye, Shades! ye're greedy aye
> To grab at aught that's brave and bonny.

> Puir, foolish, fondling, bonnie bird,
> Ye little ken what wark ye're leavin' :
> Ye've gar'd my lassie's een grow red,
> Those bonnie een grow red wi' grievin'.

That the Romantic poets turn to Catullus so little is surprising.  Wordsworth, like Milton, we should not expect to have been sympathetic to him.  Coleridge translated one poem (no. 15), and also experimented in what he calls 'Catullian Hendecasyllables'.

Keats has sometimes been compared to Catullus, but the comparison does not extend far beyond the fact that Keats also was deeply affected by the death of a brother, and shortly afterwards fell in love with a woman through whose inspiration came his greatest period of poetic creation.  His alternating moods of love and jealousy, of ecstasy and torment and finally despair have a similarity to the tragic love-affair of Catullus.

Shelley, who found inspiration in so many of the classical poets, and who read right through Livy and Lucretius, and made translations from Virgil, never mentions Catullus's name.  The lines from his poem *To Constantia Singing* are more likely to have been suggested by Sappho's poem than by Catullus's translation of it (poem 12).

> My brain is wild, my breath comes quick—
> The blood is racing in my frame,
> And thronging shades, fast and thick,
> Fall on my over-flowing eyes :
> My heart is grieving like a flame ;
> As morning dew, that in the sunbeam dies,
> I am dissolved in these consuming ecstasies.

Byron translated this poem, as well as *Lugete, O Veneres* (poem 14).

Macaulay loved Catullus, and said of him, ' I have pretty near learned all that I like best in Catullus.  He grows on me with intimacy . . . there are chords of my mind which he touches as nobody else does.  The first lines of *Miser Catulle* ;  the lines to Cornificius, written evidently from a sick-bed ;  and part of the poem beginning *Siqua recordanti*, affect me more than I can explain.  They always move me to tears '.[1]

Thomas Hardy translated the *Sirmio* poem (no. 41) as did also Calverley into a sonnet which is printed on page 89.

R. L. Stevenson wrote a poem on the subject of a disused boat, which begins :

> On the great streams the ships may go
> About men's business to and fro ;
> But I, the egg-shell pinnace, sleep
> On crystal waters ankle-deep,

which makes an interesting comparison with Catullus's *Old Yacht* (poem 42).  A version by James Elroy Flecker of this poem is given on page 89.

Swinburne also admired Catullus, and wrote a poem to him in Latin as well as another in English, and in his Elegy to Baudelaire, *Ave atque Vale*, the Roman poet speaks again :

> For thee, O now a silent soul my brother,
> Take at my hands this garland, and farewell.

In modern poetry the influence of Catullus has not been conspicuous, but J. C. Squire has written a poem to him, and Laurence Binyon's *Sirmione* describes a visit to ' the old ruined walls ' that some have thought to be the remains of Catullus's villa :

> Here, where we know what wild flowered bushes cloak
> Old ruined walls, and crumbling arches choke
> With mounded earth, though buried from our eyes
> In dark now, as beneath dark centuries

[1] v. *Catullus and his Influence* by K. P. Harrington, to which book several references in this Introduction are due.

That marble-towered magnificence of Rome,
From whose hot dust the passionate poet fled
Hither, and laid his head
Where these same waters laughed him welcome home.

But the greatest tribute to Catullus in English literature comes from the pen of Tennyson. He imitated several of the metres of Catullus, including the metre of *Collis o Heliconii* in his *Jubilee Ode*. His hendecasyllables trip as lightly as those of his master :

> Look, I come to the test, a tiny poem
> All composed in a metre of Catullus. . . .

The following poem, written after his visit to Catullus's villa at Sirmio, expresses the deep affection that he felt for the ' tenderest of Roman poets, nineteen hundred years ago ' :

> Row us out from Desenzano, to your Sirmione row!
> So they row'd, and there we landed—' O venusta Sirmio! '
> There to me thro' all the groves of olive in the summer
>     glow,
> There beneath the Roman ruin where the purple flowers
>     grow,
> Came that ' Ave atque Vale ' of the Poet's hopeless woe,
> Tenderest of Roman poets nineteen-hundred years ago,
> ' Frater Ave atque Vale '—as we wander'd to and fro
> Gazing at the Lydian laughter of the Garda Lake below
> Sweet Catullus's all-but-island, olive-silvery Sirmio!

# CHAPTER I

## CATULLUS AND HIS CIRCLE

In Northern Italy near the lovely Lake Garda lies the city of Verona, into whose first-century-A.D. amphitheatre gay Italians throng on warm evenings to see operas. It is rich in historical and literary associations, the birthplace of Pliny the Elder and Paolo Veronese the painter, and the residence of the Gothic emperor Theodoric. Its inhabitants are true Italians, quick in temper, warm in friendship, passionate in love. From here, the town of Capulet, Mercutio and Romeo, came the lyric poet, Caius Valerius Catullus.

Catullus was born in B.C. 84, the son of a comparatively wealthy man, a friend of Caesar, who owned a villa at Sirmio on Lake Garda. Already, when at sixteen he donned the white toga of manhood, Catullus had written a few juvenile poems which had attracted the attention of Cornelius Nepos, the Roman biographer, to whom he affectionately dedicates his volume. It was inevitable that the young man should seek the brilliant society of Rome, where his talents might be displayed to better advantage. We see him, therefore, at the age of twenty-two leaving for the capital, furnished with introductions to everybody of importance, perhaps from Caesar, towards whom he affected a rather studied indifference, and from Cicero, to whom he handsomely acknowledges an obligation.

The year 62 B.C. was an exciting one for Rome. Cicero's great consulship over, Catiline was killed early in the year fighting desperately at the head of his insurgents. Pompey was winning fame and empire in the East, while Caesar was on the threshold of a great military career. Yet it was not

in politics that Catullus's real interest lay.  It is true that
he attacks Caesar and Mamurra, his favourite, in several
epigrams, but the reason was probably personal, and there
may have been some jealousy underlying these virulent out-
bursts.  A reference to Caesar in a later poem suggests a
reconciliation.  Suetonius tells us that Caesar treated him
with unfailing courtesy.  It was, however, with the orators,
poets and historians of the day that Catullus formed his
warmest friendships, and it is from poems addressed to these
that we can gather much about Catullus himself and con-
temporary life at Rome.

Chief, perhaps, of his friends, and the one with whom he
is most frequently coupled, was C. Licinius Calvus, orator
and poet, a little fellow of unlimited ferocity in rhetoric
Catullus good-humouredly expostulates with him when he
sends him a book of bad verse, he spends the day with him
at literary trifling and then finds he cannot sleep, he thanks
him for his attack on the hated Vatinius, and condoles with
him on the loss of his wife Quintilia.  Another friend was
C. Helvius Cinna, for whose poem *Smyrna*, which took nine
years to write, Catullus expresses the warmest admiration.
He was probably the Cinna whom the crowd tore to pieces
in mistake for the conspirator Cinna at the assassination of
Julius Caesar (see Shakespeare's *Julius Caesar*).  To Horta-
lus (who was probably Hortensius, Cicero's chief rival at
the bar) Catullus sends a poem introducing his translation
of a poem of Callimachus, a Greek poet of the third century
B.C. and chief librarian at Alexandria, and telling of his
brother's death.  Other friends of Catullus were Veranius
and Fabullus, who went to Spain in the retinue of the
governor Piso, and whom he warns not to expect any favours
from the rascally governor, quoting his own bitter experi-
ence.  His epigrams reveal his impatience at the bad verse
of a Suffenus, his boredom at the bad oratory of a Sestius,
and his indignation at the bad characters of men like
Aurelius and Furius.

It was among such society as this that Catullus spent four

or five years in Rome. We see him as a gay young man-about-town when things went well, but disgruntled and cynical when times were bad and friends failed to come up to expectations. At one time hard up, at another cursing himself for an idle rogue, laid up with an attack of influenza, or ridiculing the foibles of a foreign Egnatius or a cockney Arrius, Catullus extracted from city life all the interest and enjoyment its infinite variety could afford.

The deep shadow cast over his life by his attachment to Clodia, sister of the infamous Publius Clodius, whom he calls Lesbia, is described in later chapters. It was this and the heavy blow he sustained by the death of his brother that made him decide to seek a change and in 57 B.C. join the staff of Memmius, who was sent out as a propraetor of Bithynia. On his way he visited the tomb of his brother in the Troad, to which visit we are indebted for the immortal elegy no. 39. He returned from Bithynia poorer in pocket, but enriched with experience both of travel and of the ways of provincial governors. His home-coming to Sirmio is expressed in a poem (no. 41), which is one of the gems of Latin literature. He was not, however, to live long after this. Some lines in a rather petulant vein (no. 46) to his poet friend Cornificius speak of his sickness both of body and mind. He died in 54 B.C. in his thirtieth year, like Shelley, and in him the Roman world lost a poet of exquisite pathos and tenderness, the equal of whom she was never again to see.

## 1 (1)  DEDICATION

Cui dono lepidum novum libellum
arido modo pumice expolitum?
Corneli, tibi : namque tu solebas

1 (1) Catullus dedicates his book to his old friend Cornelius Nepos. 2 **pumice**, pumice was used for smoothing the surface of papyrus and the edges of the roll. 3 **Corneli**, Cornelius Nepos, a fellow-countryman of Catullus, wrote Lives of famous Greeks and Romans. His 3-volumed World History (*Chronica*), now lost, was being used as a school text-book up to the 4th century A.D.

meas esse aliquid putare nugas,
jam tum cum ausus es unus Italorum          5
omne aevum tribus explicare chartis
doctis, Juppiter, et laboriosis.
quare habe tibi quicquid hoc libelli,
qualecumque ;  quod, o patrona virgo,
plus uno maneat perenne saeclo.          10


## 2   (XIII)

*Each guest brought his dish and the feast was united.*
                                        GOLDSMITH

Cenabis bene, mi Fabulle, apud me
paucis, si tibi di favent, diebus,
si tecum attuleris bonam atque magnam
cenam, non sine candida puella
et vino et sale et omnibus cachinnis.          5
haec si, inquam, attuleris, venuste noster,
cenabis bene :  nam tui Catulli
plenus sacculus est aranearum.
sed contra accipies meros amores
seu quid suavius elegantiusve est :          10
nam unguentum dabo, quod meae puellae
donarunt Veneres Cupidinesque,

**5 jam tum cum** . . . ' As long ago as when . . .'.  **8 quicquid** . . .
**qualecumque,** ' whatever it is worth . . . such as it is '.  **9 patrona
virgo,** i.e. the Muse.

**2 (XIII).**  A jocular invitation to Fabullus to dinner on condition
that he provide his own refreshment and entertainment.  All
Catullus can provide is the perfume.
**5 sale,** ' wit '.  **omnibus cachinnis,** ' all kinds of laughter '.
**9 meros amores,** ' love's very essence '.  **11 unguentum,** oint-
ment was used for anointing the diners.  Petronius tells us of a
banquet where slaves anointed the feet of the guests.  The Greeks
were said to have a different kind of ointment for every part of
the body.  **12 Veneres Cupidinesque.**  Although there was more
than one Venus and Cupid, Catullus probably uses this expression

quod tu cum olfacies, deos rogabis,
totum ut te faciant, Fabulle, nasum.


## 3   (XII)

*This here warmint's prigged your wipe.*
Ingoldsby Legends

Marrucine Asini, manu sinistra
non belle uteris in joco atque vino :
tollis lintea neglegentiorum.
hoc salsum esse putas? fugit te, inepte :
quamvis sordida res et invenusta est.                    5
non credis mihi? crede Pollioni
fratri, qui tua furta vel talento
mutari velit : est enim leporum
disertus puer ac facetiarum.
quare aut hendecasyllabos trecentos                    10
exspecta, aut mihi linteum remitte ;
quod me non movet aestimatione,
verum est mnemosynum mei sodalis.


to denote the goddess of Love generally.  She was said to have an ointment of her own called ' Kallos ' (Beauty).

3   (XII)   A protest to a friend who stole a dinner napkin.  Romans used to bring their own napkins to a dinner, and such petty pilfering was not uncommon.  The poet Martial tells us of a man who became so notorious for this practice that on his approach sailors used to reef their sails.
1 **Asinius** was the brother of Pollio, the famous friend of Horace and Virgil.  His countrymen, the Marrucini, were proverbially famed for their honesty.  **sinistra.**  It was polite to use the right hand only for eating.  The left, being in concealment, was being used by Asinius in a very ungentlemanly (*non belle*) fashion.
4 **fugit te,** ' you are mistaken '.  7 **talento,** any large sum.  We should say a thousand pounds.  8 **velit,** potential.  **leporum, facetiarum,** objective genitives depending on **disertus.**  ' With a flow of wit and humour '.  12 **aestimatione,** abl. of cause, ' for what it is worth '.  13 **verum,** ' but '.  Distinguish from *vere* and *vero.*

nam sudaria Saetaba ex Hiberis
miserunt mihi muneri Fabullus                    15
et Veranius :  haec amem necesse est
ut Veraniolum meum et Fabullum.


### 4  (IX)  VERANIUS, WELCOME HOME!

Verani, omnibus e meis amicis
antistans mihi milibus trecentis,
venistine domum ad tuos Penates
fratresque unanimos anumque matrem?
venisti.   o mihi nuntii beati!                    5
visam te incolumem audiamque Hiberum
narrantem loca, facta, nationes,
ut mos est tuus, applicansque collum
jucundum os oculosque suaviabor.
o quantum est hominum beatiorum,                   10
quid me laetius est beatiusve?


### 5  (XLIX)  TO CICERO—A COMPLIMENT

Disertissime Romuli nepotum,
quot sunt quotque fuere, Marce Tulli,

14 **sudaria**, almost the same as handkerchiefs.  **Saetaba**, from
*Saetabis* in Spain (Hiberia).  Fabullus and Veranius were in Piso's
retinue in Spain.  15 **muneri**, ' as a gift '.  17 **ut**, ' just as ', does
not, **of course**, govern *amem*.  **Veraniolum**.  Catullus loves
diminutives, which he uses to express intimacy and affection, as
we say ' Paddy ' for ' Patrick '.

4 (IX)  Veranius, having returned from Spain, is given a warm
welcome by Catullus.

3 **Penates**, gods of the storehouse, and so of the home in general.
4 **unanimos**, ' loving '.  **anum**, ' aged '.  Usually fem. noun.
6 **visam**, ' I shall see ' (from *viso*).  **Hiberum**, gen. pl.  7 **nationes**,
' tribes '.  8 **applicans collum**, ' drawing your neck towards me '.

5 (XLIX)  A short poem of thanks to Cicero for some unknown
service.

**Romuli nepotum**, ' descendants of Romulus ', an expression

quotque post aliis erunt in annis,
gratias tibi maximas Catullus
agit pessimus omnium poeta, 5
tanto pessimus omnium poeta
quanto tu optimus omnium es patronus.


## 6 (XCIII) INDIFFERENCE

*I do not love thee, Dr. Fell*
THOMAS BROWN

Nil nimium studeo, Caesar, tibi velle placere,
nec scire utrum sis albus an ater homo.


## 7 (LI*a*)

*The pains and penalties of idleness.*
POPE

Otium, Catulle, tibi molestum est ;
otio exsultas nimiumque gestis.
otium et reges prius et beatas
perdidit urbes.

covering all Romans. 6-7 Note that there is a faintly ambiguous ring about the last two lines ; some have even suggested that they are ironical.
6 (XCIII) Catullus at first expressed indifference to Caesar, and later violently attacked him and his friend Mamurra. Caesar may have been angry with the poet at first, but we are told that he became reconciled later and asked him to dinner.
1 **nil**, 'not at all'. **velle** does not seem necessary, but the whole expression may have been colloquial. 2 **albus.** Caesar was in point of fact of a fair complexion. Addison begins his Coverley papers with the sentence : 'I have observed that a reader seldom peruses a book with pleasure till he knows whether the writer of it be a black or a fair man '.

7 (LI *a*)
2 **exsultas, gestis** are physical words indicating the jumpy, fidgety state induced by having nothing to do. 3,4 **reges, urbes.** Catullus is probably thinking of Priam of Troy and the ruined cities of Asia Minor which he visited.

## 8 (LIII)  MULTUM IN PARVO

Risi nescio quem modo e corona,
qui, cum mirifice Vatiniana
meus crimina Calvus explicasset,
admirans ait haec manusque tollens,
' di magni, salaputium disertum! '     5

## 9 (L)  ARCADES AMBO

*Et cantare pares et respondere parati.*
VIRG. *Ecl.* VII

Hesterno, Licini, die otiosi
multum lusimus in meis tabellis,
ut convenerat esse delicatos.
scribens versiculos uterque nostrum
ludebat numero modo hoc modo illoc,    5
reddens mutua per jocum atque vinum.
atque illinc abii tuo lepore
incensus, Licini, facetiisque,

8 (LIII)  A joke overheard at the expense of Catullus's diminutive friend, C. Licinius Calvus, a ferocious orator.
1 **modo,** ' lately '. **corona,** the circle of bystanders.  A class of pupils would be called *corona*. 2 **Vatiniana.**  P. Vatinius was a tool of Caesar, and an unprepossessing scamp.  Cicero had attacked him two years before, but now surprisingly defended him.  Calvus's oratory was said to have been so fierce on this occasion that Vatinius could not restrain himself in court, and leaping to his feet called out, *Rogo vos, judices, num, si iste disertus est, ideo me damnari oporteat?*  He was acquitted.  For Calvus see Introduction to this chapter and next poem. 5 **salaputium,** ' little cocky ' (W. S. Landor).

9 (L)  Having spent the day with his friend Calvus in literary amusements, Catullus cannot sleep for excitement and implores his friend to come again.
2 **tabellis,** wax-covered tablets, permitting of easy erasure. 3 **delicatos,** ' gentlemen of leisure '. 5 **numero.**  They tried the same theme in different metres. **illoc** =*illo*. 6 **reddens mutua,** capping verses in alternate lines—a game not dissimilar to our

ut nec me miserum cibus juvaret
nec somnus tegeret quiete ocellos,                    10
sed toto indomitus furore lecto
versarer, cupiens videre lucem,
ut tecum loquerer simulque ut essem.
at defessa labore membra postquam
semimortua lectulo jacebant,                    15
hoc, jucunde, tibi poema feci,
ex quo perspiceres meum dolorem.
nunc audax cave sis, precesque nostras
oramus cave despuas, ocelle,
ne poenas Nemesis reposcat a te.                    20
est vehemens dea : laedere hanc caveto.


### 10   (XCVI)

*She sorrows less she died so soon*
*Than joys your love is still alive.*
SYMONS

Si quicquam mutis gratum acceptumve sepulcris
    accidere a nostro, Calve, dolore potest,
cum desiderio veteres renovamus amores
    atque olim missas flemus amicitias,
certe non tanto mors immatura dolori est                    5
    Quintiliae, quantum gaudet amore tuo.

'Crambo'.   11 **toto**, 'from side to side'.  **indomitus**, 'uncontrollable', for he could not compose himself to sleep.  18 **cavĕ**. Note scansion.  19 **ocelle**.  *Ocellus* was used as a term of endearment like our 'apple of the eye'.  20 Catullus means that a haughty rejection (' spitting upon ') of his entreaty might bring upon his friend the retribution of the awful goddess Nemesis.

10  (XCVI)   A letter of condolence to Calvus on the loss of his wife Quintilia.
1 **sepulcris**, equivalent to ' the dead '.   3 **desiderio**, 'longing for someone absent ' (see 13. 5. note).   4 **olim missas**, 'long-lost '.

## 11 (LXV)  TO HORTALUS

### LINES WRITTEN IN AFFLICTION

Etsi me assiduo confectum cura dolore
  sevocat a doctis, Hortale, virginibus,
nec potis est dulces Musarum expromere fetus
  mens animi, tantis fluctuat ipsa malis :
namque mei nuper Lethaeo gurgite fratris     5
  pallidulum manans alluit unda pedem,
Troia Rhoeteo quem subter litore tellus
  ereptum nostris obterit ex oculis—
alloquar, audiero numquam tua facta loquentem,
  numquam ego te, vita frater amabilior,     10
aspiciam posthac? at certe semper amabo,
  semper maesta tua carmina morte canam,

11 (LXV)  This poem is addressed to Hortalus, probably the same person as Hortensius, who was Cicero's famous rival at the bar. Hortalus seems to have requested that Catullus should send him a translation of Callimachus's poems. Catullus writes to say that although his mind is racked with grief at the loss of his brother, nevertheless he will comply with the request, and at the same time he sends the translation of the Alexandrine's difficult poem *The Lock of Berenice*.

1 **Etsi . . .**  As it stands the construction of this sentence is twice interrupted : 1-4 Although grief distracts my thoughts from poetry, 5-8 for my brother is dead, 9-14 I shall always mourn thee, my brother, 15-16 nevertheless, I send you the poem you require. 2 **doctis virginibus,** the Muses. 3 **expromere fetus.** Although *expromere* is frequently used for verbal utterance the metaphor here seems to be that of putting forth fruits. 4 **mens.** Translate ' thoughts '. **ipsa.** It has its own troubles without the additional cares of composition. 5 **mei fratris.** The death of Catullus's brother, who was buried in the Troad, was a blow from which Catullus never seemed to recover. Cf. poems 38, 39. **Lethaeo gurgite.** The river Lethe, one of the rivers of the underworld like the Styx, is here representative of death generally, without particular reference to the oblivion which its waters were supposed to impart. 6 **manans,** ' slow-flowing ', ' sluggish '. 7 **Rhoeteum** is a promontory of the Troad. 9 **audiero.** The future perfect is closely associated with the future *alloquar*. Shall I never hear you

qualia sub densis ramorum concinit umbris
  Daulias, absumpti fata gemens Ityli—
sed tamen in tantis maeroribus, Hortale, mitto       15
  haec expressa tibi carmina Battiadae,
ne tua dicta vagis nequiquam credita ventis
  effluxisse meo forte putes animo,
ut missum sponsi furtivo munere malum
  procurrit casto virginis e gremio,       20
quod miserae oblitae molli sub veste locatum,
  dum adventu matris prosilit, excutitur :
atque illud prono praeceps agitur decursu,
  huic manat tristi conscius ore rubor.

and (when I have heard) speak to you?  14 **Daulias,** *adj.*, sc. *ales*. Daulis was a town in Phocis, the king of which was Tereus, who by his wife Procne had a son Itys or Itylus.  When Tereus forsook his wife for her sister Philomela, telling her that Procne was dead, the two sisters conspired to kill his son Itys and serve him up for a meal to the faithless king.  The enraged Tereus pursued the sisters with an axe.  Tereus, however, was changed by the gods into a hoopoe, Procne into a swallow, and Philomela into a nightingale who ever laments the lost Itys.  The legend is referred to in Swinburne's fine chorus in *Atalanta in Calydon*.  16 **expressa,** ' translated '.  **Battiadae.**  Callimachus was a descendant of Battus of Cyrene.  17 **nequiquam** amplifies *credita ventis*. **tua dicta,** i.e. Hortalus's request.  19 Catullus likens the slipping of Hortalus's request, a token of his affection, from his mind to the love-gift of an apple falling from the bosom of a young girl as she goes to meet her mother.  Apples were frequent lovers' gifts, cf. Virg. *Ecl.* 3. 64, *malo me Galatea petit*.  21 **miserae.**  To be taken closely with **oblitae.**  23-4 Notice the contrast between **huic** (the girl) and **illud** (the apple).

# CHAPTER II

## LESBIA—HAPPINESS

WHEN Catullus was about twenty-two, he came to Rome, and met the famous Clodia, a woman seven years older than himself, and fell deeply in love. She was a member of the aristocratic Claudian family, and the wife of Metellus Celer, a heavy and stupid man who had been elected consul for the following year.

The Claudian family had a long record of service to the State, but they were proud, they held public opinion in disdain, and hated the Plebeians with an almost fanatical intensity. One ancestor, Appius Claudius, the blind censor, had built the Appian Way, and it was due to the conduct of another Claudius that the Plebs of Rome first made an effort to escape from the city, and marched to the Sacred Mount to found a new settlement. Clodia's brother, Clodius, was something of a political racketeer. He had no statesmanlike qualities, but possessed a flair for organising young men into groups or ' gangs ', which terrorised the leading members of opposing parties during Caesar's absence from Rome. Cicero, who was at one time on friendly terms with Clodia, fell foul of her brother, and attacks both of them in a speech, *Pro Caelio*, in which he can find no words bitter enough to describe them. We have, however, only his point of view ; the case for the defence has not come down to us, but it seems that Clodia's reputation in Rome was none of the best, and that she was, at least, a dangerous person.

We have no description of her. Cicero mentions her ' great blazing eyes ' (*flagrantes oculos*), and he should have known, for at one time he contemplated divorcing his wife

Terentia in her favour. In one poem, XLIII, which has not been included in this book, Catullus compares her with a lady who had 'neither a tiny nose, nor a pretty foot, nor black eyes, nor long fingers', from which we may infer that Clodia had, though this does not tell us much. But there is no doubt that she was a brilliant and fascinating woman, and an inspiration to the young men of the New Poets' circle. 'Perhaps she had more good qualities than the nettled Cicero allows, to have inspired so great a love in Catullus.'

Infatuated at first sight, but uncertain how his advances would be received, Catullus sends her his first love letter in the form of a translation of a poem of Sappho (poem 12), the Greek poetess who lived in Lesbos in the 7th century B.C., after whom he gives Clodia the name of 'Lesbia'. In no poem does he call her by her real name. There is no record of her reception of this poem, but it seems to have been favourable, for it is soon followed by others. Clodia was doubtless flattered by the young poet's admiration, and probably bored by her grave husband. The next poem (13) is written to her pet bird (perhaps a song-thrush). Catullus wishes she might play with him, as she does with the bird, and heal his heart of heavy cares. In poem 14 the bird is dead, and Catullus reveals his fondness ·for Clodia in the seriousness with which he takes her loss. It must have pleased her that he sympathised so charmingly with what other men might have regarded as a trivial incident, but in the intoxication of first love no experience is too trivial for lovers to share. Two more poems written at this period (15 and 16) picture the lovers as showering kisses upon each other in happy disregard of what the world may say. Time is passing, rosebuds must be gathered before the darkness of an endless night. In poem 17 he contrasts her beauty with that of a rival named Quintia, 'fair and tall and straight', but his 'Lesbia' possesses grace as well as beauty and 'has stolen every charm from every woman for herself alone'. In poem 18. written in the simplest language, he declares that he loves her with a devotion greater than man ever gave to woman. These poems have been described as the 'expression of a direct and personal emotion unsurpassed not only in Latin, but in any other literature'.

## 12 (LI) A FIRST LOVE-LETTER

Ille mi par esse deo videtur,
ille, si fas est, superare divos,
qui sedens adversus identidem te
    spectat et audit

dulce ridentem, misero quod omnes      5
eripit sensus mihi : nam simul te,
Lesbia, aspexi, nihil est super mi
    vocis in ore ;

lingua sed torpet, tenuis sub artus
flamma demanat, sonitu suopte      10
tintinant aures, gemina teguntur
    lumina nocte.

## 13 (II) LESBIA'S PET BIRD

Passer, deliciae meae puellae,
quocum ludere, quem in sinu tenere,

12 (LI) A free translation of a poem of Sappho to a girl of Lesbos (hence 'Lesbia', l. 7, the name Catullus gives to Clodia. For Greek original and translation, v. Appendix, p. 86.
1 **mi** =*mihi*. 5 **dulce**, 'sweetly', neuter of the adjective used adverbially. **quod**, 'a thing which'. 6 **simul** =*simul ac*. 7 **est super** =*superest*, 'remains'. **nihil** and **vocis** should be taken together. 10 **suopte**, emphatic form of *suo* in older Latin. 11 **gemina**, made to agree with *nocte*, but in sense it goes with *lumina* : 'both my eyes are sealed in darkness'.

13 (II)
1 **deliciae** (f. pl.), 'pet'. 2 **sinus**, 'bosom', 'lap'. **ludere**,

Nat. Mus. Athens. Photo by G. M. Young

GREEK GIRLS PLAYING WITH A PET BIRD

"*Passer, deliciæ meæ puellæ*" (poems 13 and 14)

VERONA, THE BIRTHPLACE OF CATULLUS, SHOWING ITS ROMAN AMPHITHEATRE

cui primum digitum dare adpetenti
et acres solet incitare morsus,
cum desiderio meo nitenti       5
carum nescioquid libet jocari,
tecum ludere, sicut ipsa, possem       9
et tristes animi levare curas!       10

## 14  (III)  THE BIRD DIES

*But have not little maidens gone,*
*And Lesbia's sparrow—all alone?*

       O. St. J. Gogarty

Lugete, o Veneres Cupidinesque,
et quantum est hominum venustiorum.
passer mortuus est meae puellae,
passer, deliciae meae puellae,
quem plus illa oculis suis amabat:       5
nam mellitus erat suamque norat
ipsam tam bene quam puella matrem.

**tenere,** and **dare** (l. 3), inf. after **solet** (l. 4). **3 primum digitum,** 'finger tip', *not* 'first finger'; cf. **summus mons. adpetenti,** 'peck'. **5 desiderium.** There is no equivalent in English for this word. You cannot have a *desiderium* for a Rolls-Royce unless you have had one and been forced to sell it. Newman had a *desiderium* for the 'angel faces ... loved long since and lost awhile'. **nitenti,** not from *nītor*, but from *nĭteo*. **desiderio meo nitenti,** 'my radiant heart's desire', i.e. *meae puellae.* **9 ludere ... possem.** Note force of the impf. 'Would that I might have had the chance to play'. The usual *utinam* is omitted.

**14 (III)** This poem has been translated by many writers, including Byron. Perhaps the best translation is into the language of Burns, **v. p. 19.**
**1 Veneres Cupidinesque,** 'Goddess of love and her attendant Cupids' (cf. poem 2, line **12** note). **2 quantum ... hominum** = *tot quot sunt homines.* The neuter of the adj. with the gen. of the noun is frequently used by Catullus instead of the adj. and noun in agreement. **venustiorum,** 'lovable', carrying on the idea contained in *Veneres.* **6 mellitus,** 'honey-sweet'. **norat,** contraction for *noverat.* **6, 7 suam ipsam,** 'his mistress'. Servants spoke of their mistress as *ipsa,* which was colloquially pronounced *issa.*

nec sese a gremio illius movebat,
sed circumsiliens modo huc modo illuc
ad solam dominam usque pipilabat.          10
qui nunc it per iter tenebricosum
illuc, unde negant redire quemquam.
at vobis male sit, malae tenebrae
Orci, quae omnia bella devoratis :
tam bellum mihi passerem abstulistis.      15
vae factum male!   vae miselle passer!
tua nunc opera meae puellae
flendo turgiduli rubent ocelli.


## 15   (v)

*Come, live with me and be my love.*
MARLOWE

Vivamus, mea Lesbia, atque amemus,
rumoresque senum severiorum
omnes unius aestimemus assis.
soles occidere et redire possunt :
nobis cum semel occidit brevis lux,        5
nox est perpetua una dormienda..
da mi basia mille, deinde centum,
dein mille altera, dein secunda centum,
deinde usque altera mille, deinde centum.
dein, cum milia multa fecerimus,           10

12 cf. *Hamlet*: ' That undiscovered country from whose bourne
No traveller returns '.   13 **at male sit**, ' Out!  A curse on you! '
*at* used to introduce imprecations.  **sit**, subj. expressing a wish.
14 **Orcus**, ' Lower World '.   16, 18 **miselle, turgiduli, ocelli.**
Catullus often uses diminutives, to express affection or pity, as we
say ' poor little . . .'   17 **tua . . . opera.**  Not plur. of *opus* but abl.
sing. of first declension word *opera*, ' by your doing ', ' because of
you '.

15   (v)   This poem and the next were adapted by Ben Jonson.
See page 87.
3 **assis**, gen. of price.  The *as* was a copper coin worth a little more
than a farthing.  **9 usque**, ' continuously ', ' without interruption '.

conturbabimus illa, ne sciamus,
aut ne quis malus invidere possit,
cum tantum sciat esse basiorum.


## 16  (VII)  HOW MANY KISSES?

*For God's sake hold your tongue, and let me love.*
DONNE

Quaeris, quot mihi basiationes
tuae, Lesbia, sint satis superque.
quam magnus numerus Libyssae harenae
lasarpiciferis jacet Cyrenis,
oraclum Jovis inter aestuosi                               5
et Batti veteris sacrum sepulcrum ;
aut quam sidera multa, cum tacet nox,
furtivos hominum vident amores ;
tam te basia multa basiare
vesano satis et super Catullo est,                         10
quae nec pernumerare curiosi
possint nec mala fascinare lingua.

11 **conturbo**, ' confuse ', i.e. mix them up and lose count.  It was
considered bad luck to count your blessings too accurately.   12 **in-
videre**, more than ' envy ' here ;  ' to cast an evil eye upon '.
13 **cum**, causal.

16  (VII)
3 **Libyssae**, ' Libyan '.   4 **lasarpiciferis ... Cyrenis.  Cyrene**,
the capital of Libya, was founded by Battus (l. 6) and was the centre
of the silphium trade. **lasarpiciferis**, ' silphium-bearing '.  The
juice (lasar) of silphium was the ancient quinine.  5 **oraclum
Jovis**, an oracle of Jupiter at Ammon, in the Libyan desert, visited
by Alexander. **inter** governs **oraclum** and **sepulcrum**.   10 **ves-
anus**, ' madly in love '.   11 **curiosi**, ' inquisitive '.   12 **fascinare**,
' bewitch '.  A *fascinum* is a charm in the form of little beads like
eyes, still worn in the Greek Islands to repel witchcraft. **mala
lingua**, nominative, subject of *possit* understood.  The evil tongue
was believed to ' cast a spell ' just as the ' evil eye ' in the last poem.

## 17 (LXXXVI) CATULLUS COMPARES A CERTAIN QUINTIA WITH LESBIA

Quintia formosa est multis: mihi candida, longa,
    recta est :  haec ego sic singula confiteor.
totum illud formosa nego :  nam nulla venustas,
    nulla in tam magno est corpore mica salis.
Lesbia formosa est, quae cum pulcherrima tota est   5
    tum omnibus una omnes surripuit Veneres.

## 18 (LXXXVII)

*My true love hath my heart.*
SIDNEY

Nulla potest mulier tantum se dicere amatam
    vere, quantum a me Lesbia amata mea es.
Nulla fides nullo fuit umquam in foedere tanta,
    quanta in amore tuo ex parte reperta mea est.

17 (LXXXVI)
2 **recta**, ' straight '.  **singula**, ' separately '.  3 **illud formosa,**
' that word " beautiful " '.  **venustas**, ' charm ', ' grace '.  4 **mica
salis**, ' grain of salt ', i.e. ' wit '.  5, 6 **cum . . . tum**, ' not only . . .
but also '.  6 **Veneres**, ' graces '.  v. poem 3, line 1.  **una**, nom. fem.,
' alone '.

18 (LXXXVII)
3 **nulla . . . nullo.**  The second negative intensifies, not cancels,
the first—a Greek construction.  **foedere**, ' bond '.  4 **in amore
tuo**, ' in my love for you '.  Take **ex parte mea** together.

# CHAPTER III

## CATULLUS AT ROME

As Catullus was a poet of changing moods, so his poetry reflects the variety of the city life wherein he found so much enjoyment. All roads led to Rome, and along its narrow streets crowded a cosmopolitan throng that provided ample material for his versatile pen. Here his observant eye would note a swarthy Spaniard whose pride in the whiteness of his teeth led him to smile broadly on all occasions in and out of season, at a funeral or the most moving part of a counsel's address to the jury; there his ear would reverberate with the superfluous aspirates of the equivalent of our Cockney 'Arry, whose aitches ruffled the billowy Ionic sea. When a Sestius publishes a frigid speech Catullus laments that it was such a frost that it gave him an attack of influenza. When a Suffenus attempts to write verse with all the equipment but none of the inspiration of a poet, Catullus, while pointing the finger of scorn at his unfortunate fellow-bard, good-humouredly remarks that we are all blind to our own failings.

It is true that the times in which Catullus lived were politically exciting, yet for a young aristocratic Roman there were sufficient distractions in city life, apart from politics, to keep him very busy. If he were not engaged in some routine affair of his household, looking after a friend's or client's affairs, attending the manumission of a slave, or witnessing a will, we might find him at the betrothal of such lovers as Septimius and Acme, of whose courtship Catullus writes with such tenderness. Or again, if he were not in the Forum listening to the city gossip or hearing the eloquent denunciations of a Calvus, Hortensius, or Cicero, we might find him attending the Games or a festival where he could hear a chorus of boys and girls singing a Hymn to Diana. The evening, too, might be occupied at a banquet with Fabullus, or at literary diversions with a boon companion like Licinius Calvus, but on a special occasion he might join the happy crowd which by the light of blazing torches conducted a radiant Vinia, resplendent in her white tunic, orange veil and yellow shoes, to the home of her future husband, Manlius, while the boys sang a Hymeneal chant foretelling health, happiness, and a fruitful issue to their wedlock.

Such was the town life which Catullus lived. Yet, when in the dogdays Rome became no place to live in, he would fly to his Tiburtine villa (Sabine villa, if you wanted to be rude!) where the cooler breezes blew, breezes that Catullus was wont to term 'plaguy blasts' when they blew to the tune of 15,000 sesterces in mortgage, a veritable 'overdraught', as it has been neatly translated. For, wealthy as his father was, he, no less than Caesar and many another young buck at Rome, sometimes found himself in debt and his purse full of cobwebs. But whether it be in this mood of comic self-commiseration, or the mood of half-serious indignation at the indifference of the old boor of Colonia to the flirtations of his pretty young wife, or most of all in the Lamb-like tenderness and simplicity of some of the passages from the two Epithalamia, Catullus remains a character to inspire our affection as much for his weaknesses as for his virtues. By reading such Latin as this we can get more directly to the heart of the Roman than by reading many pages of Caesar or Livy; and it is as important to know who the people were who conquered the ancient world as how they did it.

## 19 (XXXIV) OUR LADY OF THE CROSSWAYS

| | | |
|---|---|---|
| *Pueri et puellae* | Dianae sumus in fide<br>puellae et pueri integri :<br>Dianam pueri integri<br>    puellaeque canamus. | |
| *Puellae* | o Latonia, maximi<br>magna progenies Jovis,<br>quam mater prope Deliam<br>    deposivit olivam, | 5 |
| *Pueri* | montium domina ut fores<br>silvarumque virentium<br>saltuumque reconditorum<br>    amniumque sonantum. | 10 |
| *Puellae* | tu Lucina dolentibus<br>Juno dicta puerperis,<br>tu potens Trivia et notho es<br>    dicta lumine Luna. | 15 |
| *Pueri* | tu cursu, dea, menstruo<br>metiens iter annuum,<br>rustica agricolae bonis<br>    tecta frugibus exples. | 20 |

**19 (XXXIV)** A hymn to Diana, to be sung on some public occasion by a mixed chorus of boys and girls. Diana, whom with her brother, Apollo, Latona bore by the olive tree in the holy isle of Delos, is here praised in her three capacities, as goddess of woods and groves, as protectress of women in childbirth, and as the Moon. She is also referred to by her title Trivia, for sacred rites were paid to her as Hecate who was worshipped at cross-roads.

**1 in fide,** ' under the guardian care '. **5 Latonia,** child of Latona, i.e. Diana. **8 deposivit,** an old form of *deposuit*, ' brought forth '. **olivam.** The legend is that she grasped an olive or palm tree in her travail. **11 reconditorum.** Notice that the last syllable is elided before the vowel at the beginning of the next line. So also l. 22. **14 puerperis,** ' women in labour '. Diana was identified with Juno Lucina, **goddess of childbirth. 15 notho,** ' counterfeit ', the moon's light being borrowed.

*Pueri et*  sis quocumque tibi placet
*puellae*  sancta nomine, Romulique,
antique ut solita es, bona
sospites ope gentem.

## 20 (XXVI) CHILL WIND

Furi, villula nostra non ad Austri
flatus opposita est neque ad Favoni
nec saevi Boreae aut Apheliotae,
verum ad milia quindecim et ducentos.
o ventum horribilem atque pestilentem!  5

## 21 (XLIV) COLD-COMFORT FARM

O funde noster, seu Sabine seu Tiburs,
(nam te esse Tiburtem autumant, quibus non est
cordi Catullum laedere : at quibus cordi est,
quovis Sabinum pignore esse contendunt)
sed seu Sabine sive verius Tiburs,  5

24 **sospites,** a very old verb : religious language, cf. Eng. ' hath holpen '.

20 (XXVI) Furius had asked Catullus for a loan but Catullus pleads the mortgage on his estate as an excuse.
2 **opposita.** *Oppono* has two senses, to mortgage and to face towards. 3 **Apheliotes,** the east wind. 4 i.e. sesterces.

21 (XLIV) It seems that Sestius, who kept a good table, had invited Catullus to dinner and at the same time asked for criticism of his speech against Antius, who was a candidate for some office. At any rate, to equip himself for conversation at the table, Catullus had read the speech, which was such a frost that he pretends that it gave him a cold and that he had to fly to his villa to recuperate, without going to the dinner. Cicero refers to the poor quality of Sestius's writings.
1 **noster,** plural for singular, =*mea* as often in poetry. **Sabine.** Although the subject of *es* (understood), it is attracted into the vocative by the closeness of *funde*. **Tiburs** (Tivoli), 16 miles N.E. of Rome, where well-to-do Romans had country houses. *Tiburs* sounded more fashionable than *Sabine*. Horace on the other hand glories in the poverty of his Sabine farm. 3 **cordi est mihi,** ' I have it at heart ' ; *cordi*, perhaps locative.

fui libenter in tua suburbana
villa, malamque pectore expuli tussim,
non immerenti quam mihi meus venter,
dum sumptuosas adpeto, dedit, cenas.
nam, Sestianus dum volo esse conviva,                10
orationem in Antium petitorem
plenam veneni et pestilentiae legi.
hic me gravedo frigida et frequens tussis
quassavit usque dum in tuum sinum fugi
et me recuravi otioque et urtica.                15
quare refectus maximas tibi grates
ago, meum quod non es ulta peccatum.
nec deprecor jam, si nefaria scripta
Sesti recepso, quin gravedinem et tussim
non mi, sed ipsi Sestio ferat frigus,                20
qui tunc vocat me, cum malum librum legi.

## 22   (XLV)

*It was a lover and his lass.*

SHAKESPEARE

Acmen Septimius suos amores
tenens in gremio ' mea ' inquit ' Acme,

8, 9 The order is : *quam meus venter dedit mihi non immerenti dum adpeto sumptuosas cenas.*   11 **petitorem,** ' candidate for an office '. 13 **hic,** ' at this point '. **frequens,** tr. ' hacking '.   15 **urtica,** nettle-tea (a kind of ptisan), was known to the ancients as a cure for coughs. A good instance of zeugma, the figure of speech whereby two unrelated words are linked together, e.g. ' She went home in tears and a sedan-chair '.   17 **es ulta.**   The subject is *villa* understood.   19 **recepso,** an old form of the future perfect.   20 Notice the unexpected twist of the sentence: ' If ever I handle Sestius's poisonous stuff again I shan't raise a word of protest if the ensuing frost means a cold and a cough for—Sestius (not me) '.   21 This line implies that the invitation was conditional upon reading the speech.

22   (XLV)   A tender little poem expressing two lovers' avowal of their love under the happy auspices of a divine blessing.   For transl. v. p. 87.

1 Notice the position of the two names.   cf. *amant amantur* in l. 20 and the balance of 21-2 and 23-4.

ni te perdite amo atque amare porro  
omnes sum assidue paratus annos  
quantum qui pote plurimum perire,     5  
solus in Libya Indiaque tosta  
caesio veniam obvius leoni.'  
    hoc ut dixit, Amor, sinistra ut ante,  
    dextra sternuit approbationem.  
at Acme leviter caput reflectens,     10  
et dulcis pueri ebrios ocellos  
illo purpureo ore suaviata,  
' sic ', inquit ' mea vita Septimille,  
huic uni domino usque serviamus,  
ut multo mihi major acriorque     15  
ignis mollibus ardet in medullis '.  
    hoc ut dixit, Amor, sinistra ut ante,  
    dextra sternuit approbationem.  
nunc ab auspicio bono profecti  
mutuis animis amant amantur.     20  
unam Septimius misellus Acmen  
mavult quam Syrias Britanniasque :

3 **amare porro,** ' to go on loving '.  5 **pote,** adj., ' able '.  In full the sentence would be : *Tantum quantum pote est qui pote est plurimum perire*, lit. ' as much as he can who can love you to distraction most '.  8-9 This passage is much in dispute.  If these lines form a refrain, as they appear to do, coming twice at the end of a stanza of seven lines, it seems best to keep the same reading on each occasion.  ' As he said this, Love, as before on the left, now sneezed a " God bless you " on the right '. A sneeze was usually taken as a good omen.  Thus when Xenophon is planning the Retreat of the Ten Thousand he takes much comfort from a soldier's sneeze in the middle of his speech (*Anab*. iii. 2, 9). Catullus tells us that Love had sneezed previously on the left.  This is not so good an omen, and may imply that their love was one-sided or incomplete.  With the lovers' firm avowal of their love, a new start is made, and Love seals each affirmation with his approval. 11 **ebrios,** ' intoxicated with love ', ' swimming '.  13 **sic** with subj. followed by *ut* denotes an oath, ' So . . . may we serve . . . as I swear a flame burns . . .'  14 **domino,** i.e. Love.  22 **Syrias Britanniasque.** In the year when this poem was written, 55 B.C., Caesar made his first campaign against Britain, Crassus was setting

uno in Septimio fidelis Acme
facit delicias libidinesque.
quis ullos homines beatiores                     25
vidit, quis Venerem auspicatiorem?


## 23  (LXXXIV)  'ARRY

*'Twas whispered in Heaven, 'twas muttered in Hell.*
C. M. FANSHAWE, *Enigma on the Letter ' H '*

Chommoda dicebat, si quando commoda vellet
  dicere, et insidias Arrius hinsidias,
et tum mirifice sperabat se esse locutum,
  cum quantum poterat dixerat hinsidias.
credo, sic mater, sic Liber avunculus ejus,          5
  sic maternus avus dixerat atque avia.
hoc misso in Syriam requierant omnibus aures :
  audibant eadem haec leniter et leviter,
nec sibi postilla metuebant talia verba,
  cum subito affertur nuntius horribilis,          10
Ionios fluctus, postquam illuc Arrius isset,
  jam non Ionios esse, sed Hionios.


out for Syria, and Pompey had just exhibited 600 green-eyed lions
in the circus. It is not perhaps too fanciful to suppose that
Septimius had suggested, as any ambitious young man out to
make his fortune might, that he should join Caesar or Crassus.
Acme, we may gather, had not taken kindly to this suggestion and
a cloud had overcast their love which was dispelled when Septimius
renounced his proposal.

23 (LXXXIV) A vulgar fashion was beginning to spring up at
Rome of aspirating not merely vowels but consonants also. Cicero
also refers to the new fashion, which he deplores.
1 **commoda,** additions to soldiers' pay, ' hextras '. 4 **cum . . .
dixerat,** note pluperfect indic., ' whenever '. **quantum poterat,**
' with all the strength of his lungs '. 5 **credo,** half ironical, 'I
expect '. 7 **requierant** =*requieverant,* pluperfect of *requiesco,* ' had
begun to take a rest '. 8 **audibant** =*audiebant.*

## 24  (LXII)  EPITHALAMIUM

*Fayre childe of beauty!   Glorious lampe of love!*
SPENSER

### *Juvenes*

Vesper adest, juvenes, consurgite : Vesper Olympo
exspectata diu vix tandem lumina tollit.
surgere jam tempus, jam pingues linquere mensas ;
jam veniet virgo, jam dicetur Hymenaeus.
    Hymen o Hymenaee, Hymen ades o Hymenaee!   5

### *Puellae*

Hespere, qui caelo fertur crudelior ignis?                    20
qui natam possis complexu avellere matris,
complexu matris retinentem avellere natam,
et juveni ardenti castam donare puellam.
quid faciunt hostes capta crudelius urbe?
    Hymen o Hymenaee, Hymen ades o Hymenaee! 25

### *Juvenes*

Hespere, qui caelo lucet jucundior ignis?
qui desponsa tua firmes conubia flamma,

24   (LXII)   A marriage hymn.   The scene is a wedding feast at the
house of the bridegroom where the bride is expected shortly to arrive.
The youths are at one table and sing this Marriage Hymn in verses al-
ternately with the maidens who are at another table.   As the Evening
Star is seen the young men arise in preparation to meet the bride.
1 **Vesper,** the name of the planet Venus at evening.   *Hesperos* is its
Greek form.   **Olympo.**   Either ' from Mt. Olympus ' or ' in
heaven ' as the Romans habitually used *Olympus* for ' heaven '.
4 **dicetūr.**   A short vowel lengthened before ' h '.   This occurs
elsewhere before the word *Hymenaeus.*   5 **Hymen** (also Hymen-
aeus) was the god of marriage.   This was the cry always raised on
escorting home the bride.   6-19. In the omitted portion the maidens
hail the Star and the youths say that they will have to look to their
laurels if they are to match the maids in song.   There is a kind of
rivalry in this hymn, for it will be seen that the maids and youths
take opposite views.   **21 possis.**   Note subj., ' for thou canst '
**27 desponsa conubia,** referring to the *sponsalia,* the betrothal,
which was celebrated as a family holiday.   The father promised

quae pepigere viri, pepigerunt ante parentes,
nec junxere prius quam se tuus extulit ardor.
quid datur a divis felici optatius hora?     30
    Hymen o Hymenaee, Hymen ades o Hymenaee!

### Puellae

Ut flos in saeptis secretus nascitur hortis,     39
ignotus pecori, nullo convulsus aratro,     40
quem mulcent aurae, firmat sol, educat imber ;
multi illum pueri, multae optavere puellae :
idem cum tenui carptus defloruit ungui,
nulli illum pueri, nullae optavere puellae :
sic virgo dum intacta manet, dum cara suis est ;     45
cum castum amisit polluto corpore florem,
nec pueris jucunda manet, nec cara puellis.
    Hymen o Hymenaee, Hymen ades o Hymenaee!

### Juvenes

Ut vidua in nudo vitis quae nascitur arvo
numquam se extollit, numquam mitem educat uvam,     50
sed tenerum prono deflectens pondere corpus
jam jam contingit summum radice flagellum ;
hanc nulli agricolae, nulli coluere juvenci :
at si forte eadem est ulmo conjuncta marito,
multi illam agricolae, multi coluere juvenci :     55
sic virgo dum intacta manet, dum inculta senescit ;
cum par conubium maturo tempore adepta est,

(*despondeo*) the bride to the bridegroom, and the latter promised
to wed her, often giving her an engagement ring (*anulus pronubus*).
32-38 The text is imperfect. 39-58 One of the most famous
passages of Catullus, translated by Ben Jonson in *The Barriers*, see
p. 15. 40 **convulsus**, ' torn up '. 43 **tenui**, here ' sharp '. The
flower is nipped. 45 **dum ... dum**, ' *while* she remains un-
touched, *so long* is she dear to her own.' Similarly in line 56.
49 **vidua**. A vine which was not trained to a tree was called a
' widow ' or ' mateless ' vine. 52 **jam jam**, ' ever threatens to
touch '. **summum flagellum**, ' topmost shoot '. Notice the
inversion of the more usual *radicem flagello*.

cara viro magis et minus est invisa parenti.
Hymen o Hymenaee, Hymen ades o Hymenaee!

## 25 (xxxix) THE SPANIARD SHOWS HIS TEETH

Egnatius, quod candidos habet dentes,
renidet usquequaque.  si ad rei ventum est
subsellium, cum orator excitat fletum,
renidet ille.  si ad pii rogum fili
lugetur, orba cum flet unicum mater,                    5
renidet ille.  quicquid est, ubicumque est,
quodcumque agit, renidet.  hunc habet morbum,
neque elegantem, ut arbitror, neque urbanum.
quare monendum te est mihi, bone Egnati ;
si urbanus esses aut Sabinus aut Tiburs                 10
aut parcus Umber aut obesus Etruscus
aut Lanuvinus ater atque dentatus
aut Transpadanus, ut meos quoque attingam,
aut quilibet qui puriter lavit dentes,
tamen renidere usquequaque te nollem :                  15
nam risu inepto res ineptior nulla est.

58 **invisa,** because the parent wishes to see his line continued.
60-66 The hymn ends with an admonition to the bride regarding
her duty to her husband and her responsibility to her father.

25   (xxxix)   All sorts and conditions of men came to Rome from
the provinces, naturally not all to a Roman gentleman's taste.  Par-
ticularly offensive was Egnatius, who smiled on every possible
occasion, like Mr. Carker in *Dombey and Son*, to show off his teeth.
1 **candidos dentes.**  The Romans had many kinds of tooth powder,
mostly of crushed bones, shells or pumice.  They seem to have taken
great care of their teeth.  2 **usquequaque,** ' on all occasions '.
**rei,** from *reus*, ' defendant ', ' prisoner '.  4 **pii,** ' dutiful '.  9 **mon-
endum te est mihi.**  Notice this gerundial construction, instead of
*monendus es mihi*.  10 Catullus means that if he were a countryman
of his own of cleanly habits he still would object ; how much more
with a Spaniard of uncleanly habits.  Notice that Catullus works
outwards from Rome.  **Sabinus aut Tiburs** reminds him of his
country villa.  11 **parcus,** ' thrifty '.  12 **dentatus,** ' with a fine set
of teeth ' which his swarthy complexion would help to show.  13
**Transpadanus.**  Here Catullus comes to his home town of Verona.

## 26 (XIV)  GIFTS THAT ARE NO GIFTS

*. . . Twelve volumes, twelve of amplest size,*
*Redeemed from tapers and defrauded pies.*

POPE, *Dunciad*

Ni te plus oculis meis amarem,
jucundissime Calve, munere isto
odissem te odio Vatiniano :
nam quid feci ego quidve sum locutus
cur me tot male perderes poetis?                     5
isti di mala multa dent clienti,
qui tantum tibi misit impiorum.
quod si, ut suspicor, hoc novum ac repertum
munus dat tibi Sulla litterator,
non est mi male, sed bene ac beate,                 10
quod non dispereunt tui labores.
di magni, horribilem et sacrum libellum,
quem tu scilicet ad tuum Catullum
misti, continuo ut die periret
Saturnalibus, optimo dierum!                        15

**26** (XIV)   At the Saturnalian festival (Dec. 19th) Romans used to send each other presents in much the same way as we do at Christmas. Calvus (see poems 8 and 9) had sent Catullus a book of bad verse. Catullus threatens to retaliate in kind.
**2 jucundissime.** ' My sportive friend '. Practical jokes were the rule at the Saturnalia, and the point is that Catullus was bound by tradition to read what was sent. **3 Vatiniano,** see poem 8. This may refer to Vatinius's unpopularity (it was said of him that he had almost more enemies than lumps on his neck and feet!) ; alternatively it may refer to the violence of Calvus's attack on Vatinius. **6 isti,** dative. **clienti,** someone who had sent the volume in return for being defended by Calvus. **7 tantum impiorum,** ' such a pack of uninspired knaves '. **8 repertum,** ' studied ', ' recherché '. **9 Sulla litterator.** A freedman of the dictator Sulla whose name he took. He was a schoolmaster (*litterator* is a contemptuous word, ' an abecedarian ') and may have sought this way to repay his lawyer. **10 bene ac beate . . .** ' I congratulate you that your efforts are not wasted '. Ironical. **12 sacrum,** ' accursed ', cf. French *sacré*. **14 misti** = *misisti*. **continuo,** adv., ' at once ', ' that he might drop down dead on the spot '.

non non hoc tibi, salse, sic abibit:
nam, si luxerit, ad librariorum
curram scrinia, Caesios, Aquinos,
Suffenum, omnia colligam venena,
ac te his suppliciis remunerabor.                    20
vos hinc interea valete, abite
illuc, unde malum pedem attulistis,
saecli incommoda, pessimi poetae.

### 27   (XXII)   AN AMIABLE WEAKNESS

*Full wise is he that can himselven knowe.*
CHAUCER, *The Monkes Tale*

Suffenus iste, Vare, quem probe nosti,
homo est venustus et dicax et urbanus,
idemque longe plurimos facit versus.
puto esse ego illi milia aut decem aut plura
perscripta, nec sic ut fit in palimpsesto          5

**16 non** . . .   We should say, 'You won't get away with it like that'.
**17 si.**   Not that there was much doubt about the dawn ; perhaps it
is a superstitious way of speaking, just as some people say, 'D.V.'
**librariorum,** 'booksellers'.   **18 scrinia,** cylindrical book-boxes
for storing the rolls.   **Caesios,** etc.   Caesius and others are taken
as types of bad poets.   For Suffenus see next poem.   **22 malum
pedem,** 'your halting feet'.   There is a play on the meaning of
*pes,* which may refer also to metre.

**27   (XXII)**   Among the accomplishments of a Roman gentleman
not the least was the art of versification.   Even the busiest of men,
like the Emperor Augustus, found time for it occasionally.   Not
unnaturally some displayed more zeal than talent and, like Suffenus,
remained blind to their failing.   Suffenus is the exact opposite of
Goldsmith, of whom it was said that he 'wrote like an angel and
talked like poor Poll '.
**1 probe,** 'well'.   **nosti** = *novisti.*   **3 idem** is often used in character
studies where we should say ' at the same time '.   **longe plurimos,**
i.e. more than anyone else.   Thus the bore who inflicted himself
on Horace said : *nam quis me scribere plures aut citius possit
versus?*   Satires I. 9. 23; cf. Pope, ' Lord Fanny spins a thousand
such a day '.   **5 ut fit,** ' as often happens '.   **in palimpsesto.**

relata : chartae regiae, novi libri,
novi umbilici, lora rubra, membranae,
derecta plumbo, et pumice omnia aequata.
haec cum legas tu, bellus ille et urbanus
Suffenus unus caprimulgus aut fossor 10
rursus videtur : tantum abhorret ac mutat.
hoc quid putemus esse? qui modo scurra,
aut si quid hac re tritius, videbatur,
idem infaceto est infacetior rure,
simul poemata attigit ; neque idem umquam 15
aeque est beatus ac poema cum scribit :
tam gaudet in se tamque se ipse miratur.
nimirum idem omnes fallimur, neque est quisquam
quem non in aliqua re videre Suffenum
possis. suus cuique attributus est error : 20
sed non videmus manticae quod in tergo est.

Palimpsest was parchment which had already been written upon, and had had the writing erased. **6 regiae chartae,** ' crown paper ', the best kind of papyrus. **libri,** probably the sheets which were pasted together to make the papyrus rolls. **7 umbilici,** the knobs at the end of the stick round which the cylinder was rolled. **lora,** strings for tying round the rolls. **membranae,** parchment wrappers for holding the rolls. **8 derecta plumbo,** ' ruled with lead '— *derecta* seems to refer forwards to *omnia*. Lines were drawn on manuscripts with a circular plate of lead, guided by a ruler. **pumice,** see note on 1. 2. **10 unus caprimulgus,** lit. ' any goatherd ', so ' country bumpkin '. **fossor,** ' ditcher ' and so ' clown '. **11 abhorret,** ' he is inconsistent (with himself) '. **12 putemus,** ' what are we to think? ' (deliberative subjunctive). **scurra,** ' a wit '. **13 tritius,** a man who has had his corners rubbed off (*tero*) would be a man of the world—' practised '. **15 simul** = *simulatque*. **17 in se,** ablative, ' he is so full of himself '. **18 fallimur,** equivalent to the Greek middle voice, ' we all deceive ourselves in respect to the same thing '. **21 manticae,** a partitive genitive, ' that part of the wallet '. The idea comes from a fable of Aesop. Each man has a double wallet hanging from the shoulders, with one part in front and the other behind. In front we carry our neighbour's faults, and behind our own, not visible to ourselves. Burns's lines are famous : ' Oh wad some power the giftie gie us, To see oursels as others see us! '

## 28  (XVII)  PONS ASINI

*He heareth not, he stirreth not, he moveth not ;*
*The ape is dead. . . .*
SHAKESPEARE, *Romeo and Juliet*

O Colonia, quae cupis ponte ludere longo,
et salire paratum habes, sed vereris inepta
crura ponticuli axulis stantis in redivivis,
ne supinus eat cavaque in palude recumbat ;
sic tibi bonus ex tua pons libidine fiat,                    5
in quo vel Salisubsili sacra suscipiantur :
munus hoc mihi maximi da, Colonia, risus.
quemdam municipem meum de tuo volo ponte
ire praecipitem in lutum per caputque pedesque,
verum totius ut lacus putidaeque paludis              10
lividissima maximeque est profunda vorago.
insulsissimus est homo, nec sapit pueri instar

28  (XVII)  Catullus expresses his contempt for a fellow-country-
man who neglected his pretty wife   He wants to throw him from
the town's new bridge.
1 **Colonia,** perhaps the modern Cologna, east of Verona. **ludere,**
' to celebrate games '. 2 **paratum habes,** ' have made your prepara-
tions '.  It is from a construction like this that the beginnings of
the auxiliary verb can be seen.  **inepta,** ' ill-fitted ' and so ' crazy '
3 **axulis redivivis,** ' resurrected planks ', which had been used for
some other purpose first.  5 **ex,** ' in accordance with '.  6 **Salisub-
sili.**  Salisubsilus is said to be an epithet of Mars, meaning ' leap-
ing '.  There was a college of priests of Mars at Rome called the
*Salii,* so named from their leaping dance, who in the early part of
March made a solemn procession about the sacred parts of the city.
They carried the holy shields of Mars and chanted the *axamenta,*
religious hymns written in an obsolete and almost unintelligible
Latin.  There were similar priests of Hercules.  It is perhaps some
such ceremony that is referred to here.  Bridges were often the
scene of such rites.  Thus on the Ides of May twenty-three figures
of men, made of rushes (called *Argei*) were thrown into the river
Tiber from the Pons Sublicius, the old pile bridge at Rome.
7 **da.**  The imperative following *sic* with the subjunctive introduces
a condition to the wish—' on condition that you give . . .'  **maximi
risus,** genitive of definition—' consisting of a loud peal of laughter '.
10 **verum.**  The force is, ' only mind that it is . . .'.  **ut** must

bimuli tremula patris dormientis in ulna.
cui cum sit viridissimo nupta flore puella,
et puella tenellulo delicatior haedo,         15
asservanda nigerrimis diligentius uvis,
ludere hanc sinit ut libet, nec pili facit uni,
nec se sublevat ex sua parte, sed velut alnus
in fossa Liguri jacet suppernata securi,
tantundem omnia sentiens quam si nulla sit usquam.  20
talis iste meus stupor nil videt, nihil audit,
ipse qui sit, utrum sit an non sit, id quoque nescit.
nunc eum volo de tuo ponte mittere pronum,
si pote stolidum repente excitare veternum
et supinum animum in gravi derelinquere caeno,  25
ferream ut soleam tenaci in voragine mula.

mean ' where ' here—a rare usage, but found also in 45. 3.  **13 bim-
uli,** ' two years old '.  Notice the diminutives in this passage, and
in particular the double diminutive *tenellulo*.  These are half
colloquial, but Catullus likes them for their pathetic appeal.
**14 viridissimo flore,** ' in the freshest bloom of youth '.  Both
*viridis* and *flos* were so often used metaphorically that Catullus here
apparently loses sight of their literal meaning.  **15 et,** equivalent to
*et quidem*, ' and yet '.  16 **nigerrimis,** i.e. ' ripest '.  17 **pili,**
genitive of value from *pilus*, a hair—hence a thing of no value.
**uni,** an old form of the genitive, for *unius*.  18 **se sublevat,** tr.
' bestir himself '.  **alnus.**  Alders were once, at any rate, frequent in
the marshy neighbourhood of the Po.  Cf. the story of Phaethon's
sisters.  19 **Liguri.**  The Ligurians were skilled woodsmen.
**suppernata,** lit. ' ham-strung ', a word that has more reference
to a human being than a tree.  20 **nulla sit,** ' as if it (the
tree) had no existence anywhere '.  This seems better than taking
**nulla as** ' she ' (the wife).  21 **talis** is used with a predicative
force—' that's the kind of man he is '.  **iste meus stupor,** abstract
for concrete—' this blockhead of mine '.  24 **pote** for *potest*.  He
(the booby) is the subject.  25 **supinum.**  Its usual sense is ' flat
on the back ', its opposite being *pronus* :  here, however, it seems to
be used in its derived sense of ' listless ', ' lazy '.

## 29 (LXI)  WEDDING SONG

*Hail, wedded love, mysterious law, true source*
*Of human offspring.*

MILTON, *Paradise Lost*, iv. 750

Hymen, god of marriage, is bidden **to a wedding,**

Collis o Heliconii
cultor, Uraniae genus,
qui rapis teneram ad virum
virginem, o Hymenaee Hymen,
   o Hymen Hymenaee,     5

arrayed **even as** a fair bride, and leading torch-bearers,

cinge tempora floribus
suave olentis amaraci,
flammeum cape, laetus huc
huc veni niveo gerens
   luteum pede soccum,     10

**to attend the** solemn nuptials of the wise Manlius and fair Vinia.

namque Vinia Manlio,     16
qualis Idalium colens
venit ad Phrygium Venus
judicem, bona cum bona
   nubet alite virgo.     20

29 (LXI)  This poem was perhaps a wedding present, written to celebrate the wedding of Catullus's friend, Manlius Torquatus with Vinia Aurunculeia.  It was to be sung, as the custom was at Rome, by a band of boys and girls carrying torches as the bride was conducted in a procession through the streets to the house of the bridegroom.

1 **Heliconii.**  Hymen, as the son of the Muse, Urania, would dwell on Mt. Helicon.  3 **rapis.**  The Roman wedding ceremony contains many allusions to the forcible abduction characteristic of more primitive times.  Typical of this is the parting of the bride's hair with a spear.  7 **suave,** neuter of the adjective used adverbially, cf. 12. 5.  8 **flammeum,** a full-length orange-coloured veil worn by brides.  10 **soccum,** a loose yellow shoe.  17 **qualis** . . . Paris, the handsome shepherd of Phrygia, when called upon to decide between the offerings of Aphrodite (Venus), Hera and Athena, awarded the golden apple of Discord to Aphrodite for her gift of a beautiful bride (Helen).  Even so, Manlius had chosen the fair Vinia. **Idalium,** a city of Cyprus, an island devoted to the worship of Venus.  19-20 **bona alite.**  Auspices were always taken before the

| | | |
|---|---|---|
| Wherefore must the god leave his wonted haunts, | quare age huc aditum ferens<br>perge linquere Thespiae<br>rupis Aonios specus,<br>nympha quos super irrigat<br>    frigerans Aganippe, | 26<br><br><br><br>30 |
| to escort the bride to the home of her love, | ac domum dominam voca<br>conjugis cupidam novi,<br>mentem amore revinciens,<br>ut tenax hedera huc et huc<br>    arborem implicat errans. | <br><br><br><br>35 |
| while maids are bidden sing a hymn to the wedding god, | vosque item simul, integrae<br>virgines, quibus advenit<br>par dies, agite in modum<br>dicite ' o Hymenaee Hymen,<br>    o Hymen Hymenaee '. | <br><br><br><br>40 |
| the peerless one, the stay of hearth and home. | nulla quit sine te domus<br>liberos dare, nec parens<br>stirpe nitier : at potest<br>**te** volente.  quis huic deo<br>    compararier ausit? | 66<br><br><br><br>70 |
| The throng are mustered with torches without Vinia's house. | claustra pandite januae,<br>virgo adest.  viden ut faces<br>splendidas quatiunt comas? | 76 |

.    .    .    .    .    .    .

wedding.  **27-8 Thespiae rupis,** i.e. Mt. Helicon.  Thespiae is a town at the south-east foot of Helicon.  Aganippe (l. 30) is a stream on the mountain said to give poetical inspiration to those who drink of it.  **31 domum voca.**  The main feature of the wedding rite was the torchlight procession when the bride was taken to her new home.  **38 par dies,** 'a like day', when they too would be wed.  **in modum,** 'in measure', 'to time'. **66 quit,** from *queo*, 'to be able'.  **68 nitier . . . compararier,** old forms of the passive infinitive.  **70 ausit,** a form of the present subjunctive of *audeo*.  **76 claustra.**  The scene shifts to the doors of the bride's house, where the company are waiting for Vinia to appear. **77 viden** = *videsne*.  **faces.**  There were five torches, three for the male, the first odd number, and two for the female, the first even.

|  |  |  |
|---|---|---|
| Yet she lingereth for modesty and regret. | tardet ingenuus pudor :<br><br>.    .    .    .    .    .<br>quem tamen magis audiens<br>   flet, quod ire necesse est. | 80 |
| But the Poet comforteth her, for she is fair, | flere desine.   non tibi, Aurunculeia, periculum est,<br>ne qua femina pulchrior<br>clarum ab Oceano diem<br>   viderit venientem. | 85 |
| fair as a flower. So he exhorteth her to come forth, | talis in vario solet<br>divitis domini hortulo<br>stare flos hyacinthinus.<br>sed moraris, abit dies :<br>   prodeas, nova nupta. | 90 |
| to see and hear the gathered company. | prodeas, nova nupta, si<br>jam videtur, et audias<br>nostra verba.   vide ut faces<br>aureas quatiunt comas :<br>   prodeas, nova nupta. | 95 |
| Boys greet the bride as she cometh forth with torches raised. | tollite, o pueri, faces :<br>flammeum video venire.<br>ite, concinite in modum<br>' io Hymen Hymenaee io,<br>   io Hymen Hymenaee '. | 117<br><br>120 |

79 The text has unfortunately some lacunae, which do not, however, greatly impair the sense. 80 **quem**, perhaps referring to *pudorem*. **magis**, i.e. ' heeding it rather than us '. 85 **clarum**. Notice that it was a fine day for a wedding. 92-3 **si jam videtur**. ' If by now you have made up your mind ', lit. ' If it now seems good to you ', implying that she had hesitated too long. 122-51 In these omitted lines the boys are called upon to scatter nuts, a usage resembling the throwing of rice at our own weddings, and to indulge in merriment and coarse jesting, accompanied by ribald verses called Fescennine, at the expense of the bridegroom, all of which were features of the ancient ceremony. The ribaldry had its religious significance. By too much happiness the bride-

<table>
<tr><td>She reacheth her new home where she will be mistress</td><td>en tibi domus ut potens<br>et beata viri tui,<br>quae tibi sine serviat<br>(io Hymen Hymenaee io,<br>   io Hymen Hymenaee),</td><td>152<br><br><br>155</td></tr>
<tr><td>all her days ;</td><td>usque dum tremulum movens<br>cana tempus anilitas<br>omnia omnibus annuit.<br>io Hymen Hymenaee io,<br>   io Hymen Hymenaee.</td><td><br><br><br>160</td></tr>
<tr><td>and is lifted over the threshold</td><td>transfer omine cum bono<br>limen aureolos pedes,<br>rasilemque subi forem.<br>io Hymen Hymenaee io,<br>   io Hymen Hymenaee.</td><td><br><br><br>165</td></tr>
<tr><td>whilst Manlius waiteth at the wedding feast.</td><td>aspice, intus ut accubans<br>vir tuus Tyrio in toro<br>totus immineat tibi.</td><td></td></tr>
</table>

groom might incur the jealousy of the gods. Such uncomplimentary remarks served as a useful corrective. **152 en tibi.** An allusion may be seen here to the following custom. When the bride reached the bridegroom's house, he always asked her, ' What is your name? ' she thereupon replied *Ubi tu Caius ego Caia*, implying that where he was lord she was mistress of the household. He then gave her the keys of the house. **ut,** ' how ', as also later. **154 sine.** This is a verb, which is followed by a subjunctive construction. **158 tempus,** ' a temple ', and so ' the head '. **159 omnia omnibus,** an amusing description of an old woman, the constant shaking of whose head suggests that she is saying ' yes ' to everybody and everything. **162 transfer.** The bride was always lifted over the threshold, perhaps another relic of forcible abduction. Sometimes the doorposts were smeared with pigs' fat and wreathed with wool. **omine cum bono.** Another explanation is that the bride was lifted over the threshold to avoid the possibility of stumbling, which of course would be a very bad omen. **164 rasilem,** ' polished '. **forem,** ' door ', usually plural. **167 aspice.** The bride now sees her husband reclining alone on his couch at the supper which preceded the wedding. Such a banquet is the scene of no. 24. **ut,** ' how '. **169 totus immineat,** ' has all his thoughts on thee '.

io Hymen Hymenaee io,                    170
io Hymen Hymenaee.

Her pages leave her, and she entereth the marriage chamber,

mitte bracchiolum teres,                 177
praetextate, puellulae :
jam cubile adeat viri.
io Hymen Hymenaee io,                    180
io Hymen Hymenaee.

where matrons place her upon the wedding-couch,

vos bonae senibus viris
cognitae bene feminae,
collocate puellulam.
io Hymen Hymenaee io,                    185
io Hymen Hymenaee.

whither cometh the bridegroom to meet her straightway,

jam licet venias, marite :
uxor in thalamo tibi est
ore floridulo nitens,
alba parthenice velut                    190
luteumve papaver.

and embraceth her openly.

non diu remoratus es,                    197
jam venis.  bona te Venus
juverit, quoniam palam
quod cupis capis et bonum                200
non abscondis amorem.

177 **mitte bracchiolum teres,** ' let go the smooth arm '.  The young boy (there were usually three) clad in the *toga praetexta* (dress of boyhood), who has been accompanying the bride was not allowed to go past the door.  178 **puellulae.**  The diminutive shows that the bride must have been very young.  179 **adeat.** She now approaches the *lectus genialis*, the marriage couch which was later placed in the *atrium* and dedicated to the *genii* or guardian spirits of the couple.  182 **vos bonae.**  She was still accompanied by her *pronubae*, the equivalent of our bridesmaids, except that they had to be long-married women who had had one husband only. 184 **collocate.**  The bride is now ceremonially laid on the couch 187 **licet,** with the subjunctive as often.  **marite,** the final ' e ' is elided before *uxor* at the beginning of the next line.  190 **parthenice, a kind of daisy.**  197 The bridegroom now comes to the

| | |
|---|---|
| But, without, the company sing of the countless joys of the bride-groom, | ille pulveris Africi<br>siderumque micantium<br>subducat numerum prius,<br>qui vestri numerare vult     205<br>   multa milia ludi. |
| and pray that his name be con-tinued | ludite ut libet, et brevi<br>liberos date.   non decet<br>tam vetus sine liberis<br>nomen esse, sed indidem     210<br>   semper ingenerari. |
| by the birth of a baby boy, a Torquatus, | Torquatus volo parvulus<br>matris e gremio suae<br>porrigens teneras manus<br>dulce rideat ad patrem     215<br>   semihiante labello. |
| like his father and mother, | sit suo similis patri<br>Manlio et facile insciis<br>noscitetur ab omnibus<br>et pudicitiam suae     220<br>   matris indicet ore. |
| as honoured in his parentage as | talis illius a bona<br>matre laus genus approbet, |

wedding-couch and takes the bride in his arms. **204 subducat numerum prius,** 'let him first count' the sands. To count the joys of Manlius is only possible for one who can first achieve the other feat. **206 ludi,** a collective noun, 'joys'. **207 brevi,** sc. *tempore.* **209-10 tam vetus nomen.** Manlius was a direct descendant of T. Manlius Torquatus, the famous warrior of early Rome. **210 indidem,** 'from the same stock'. There are many famous names like that of the Claudii that continue right through Roman history. **215 dulce.** Cf. note on *suave,* l. 7. **216 semi-hiante labello,** 'with lips half-parted'. Scan *sēm(ih)ĭantĕ.* **labello,** diminutive of *labrum.* **218 insciis,** i.e. so that strangers would recognise the likeness. **223 genus approbet,** 'establish his birth', i.e. show that he is a true son of his mother.

was Telemachus in his mother Penelope.

> qualis unica ab optima
> matre Telemacho manet    225
>     fama Penelopeo.

The guests depart while the Poet invoketh upon the wedded pair everlasting happiness.

> claudite ostia, virgines :
> lusimus satis.   at, boni
> conjuges, bene vivite et
> munere assiduo valentem    230
>     exercete juventam.

**225 Telemacho.** Telemachus in character more closely resembled his mother Penelope than his father Odysseus from whom he was so long separated. **228 lusimus satis.** This may be spoken either by Catullus or a leader of the choir. **230 munere assiduo.** Tr. ' And in constant service to Hymen employ your youth and power '.

# CHAPTER IV

## LESBIA—DOUBT

In Chapter II we read of Catullus in ' the very ecstasy of
love '. We do not know how long the period lasted when no
thoughts of the future arose to disturb the two lovers.
Catullus was utterly confident ; ' Lesbia ' loved him whole-
heartedly ; and he returned the love. In poem 30 we hear
the first jarring note of a quarrel, but if his love sometimes
' speaks sharply ' to him, so does he to her, and he knows
that ' lovers' quarrels are but a renewal of love ', as Terence
said,[1] and prays to die if he ever stops loving her.

But there is one poem (31) in which there is a shadow of
doubt. He prays the great gods that they may grant her
eternal fidelity, and that ' she may swear it with all her
heart and soul ', which is a prayer that he would have been
less likely to utter had he been sure of its fulfilment.

Catullus, however, did not find his love returned with the
same constancy, and as time passes he is plunged into fits of
increasing jealousy. What were Clodia's feelings in this
affair we are not told. At first she was doubtless flattered
by the devotion of a young poet and may have sincerely
returned the affection he gave her, but he must have been
an exacting lover and too possessive for a woman of a
temperament less constant than his own. In any case, she
finally tired of his ardour and sought for other companion-
ship. His suffering when he first realised her unfaithfulness
we can only imagine. If he expressed it in a poem, we do
not possess it. But in poem 32 he reproaches her bitterly
with the taunt that women's vows are ' writ in water and

[1] *Amantium irae amoris integratio.*

blowne away with winde ', as Donne also said. When, after three years or so, her husband Metellus dies and she is free to marry again, he realises that she has no intention of being faithful to him. He now grows more despondent and blames her because his love has degenerated into a vulgar passion. Once he loved her not only as a lover but also with the devotion of ' a father for his children '; now, although his love is as ardent as ever (*impensius uror*), he reveals in poem 33 that he no longer cares about her character. His tragedy lies in the fact that he cannot cease to desire even though he has ceased to respect her (poem 34). The two lines of simple prose, yet burning poetry, of poem 35 are the perfect expression of this conflict :

> I hate yet love her. Will you ask me why?
> I know not. But I feel. 'Tis agony.

Coleridge, too, knew this torment :

> To be wroth with one we love
> Doth work like madness in the brain.

Poem 36 is a bitter outburst against a friend, Caelius Rufus, who stole Clodia's love from him. In his disillusionment he sees his good deeds as wasted acts, and allows his faith in human nature to be weakened through the unfaithfulness of one who ' held him but lately as his one true friend '. To lose at the same time both his friend and the woman he loves drives him to despair. In poem 37 he chides himself (*miser Catulle*) for his hopeless love. Once the days were bright for him ; now the sun is set and there is nothing but darkness left. The line *fulsere quondam candidi tibi soles* contains an echo of that happy earlier poem in which the lovers grasp happiness before the coming of endless night. In this soliloquy self-pity, retrospection and a stoical resignation follow each other, but his repeated determination to stand firm betrays his real wavering :

> *at tu, Catulle, destinatus obdura.*

## 30  (XCII)

*I curse her every hour sincerely,*
*Yet, hang me, but I love her dearly.*

SWIFT

Lesbia mi dicit semper male nec tacet umquam
de me : Lesbia me dispeream nisi amat.
quo signo? quia sunt totidem mea : deprecor illam
assidue, verum dispeream nisi amo.

## 31  (CIX)

*And I will love thee still, my dear,*
*Till a' the seas gang dry.*

BURNS

Jucundum, mea vita, mihi proponis amorem
hunc nostrum inter nos perpetuumque fore.
di magni, facite ut vere promittere possit,
atque id sincere dicat et ex animo,
ut liceat nobis tota perducere vita
aeternum hoc sanctae foedus amicitiae.

5

## 32  (LXX)

*Woman's faith and woman's trust—*
*Write the characters in dust,*
*Stamp them on the running stream,*
*Print them on the moonlight's beam.*

SIR W. SCOTT

Nulli se dicit mulier mea nubere malle
quam mihi, non si se Juppiter ipse petat.

**30  (XCII)**  The first jarring note.
2 The order is, *dispeream nisi Lesbia me amat.* 3 totidem mea, sc.
some word like *verba* to agree with *mea.* The phrase is taken from
some game of chance. ' My (points) are the same number ', i.e. ' six
of one to half a dozen of the other '. **deprecor,** ' cry out against '.

**31  (CIX)**  Lesbia has promised to be true to life's end, but a faint
cloud of doubt overshadows Catullus's joy.
**5 perducere,** ' prolong ', ' continue '.

dicit : sed mulier cupido quod dicit amanti,
in vento et rapida scribere oportet aqua.


## 33   (LXXII)

*That me alone you lov'd, you once did say.*
LOVELACE

Dicebas quondam solum te nosse Catullum,
Lesbia, nec prae me velle tenere Jovem.
dilexi tum te non tantum ut vulgus amicam,
sed pater ut natos diligit et generos.
nunc te cognovi : quare etsi impensius uror,
multo mi tamen es vilior et levior.
qui potis est? inquis.   quod amantem injuria talis
cogit amare magis, sed bene velle minus.


## 34   (LXXV)

*To be wroth with one we love*
*Doth work like madness in the brain.*
COLERIDGE

Huc est mens deducta tua, mea Lesbia, culpa,
atque ita se officio perdidit ipsa suo,
ut jam nec bene velle queat tibi, si optima fias,
nec desistere amare, omnia si facias.


33  (LXXII)
1 **nosse**, contraction for *novisse*.   3 **dilexi** from *diligo*, 'to love'.
Distinguish from *deligo*, 'to choose'.   **tantum**, 'only'.   **amicam**,
'favourite'.   5 **impensius**, 'more vehemently'.   7 **qui**, 'how',
old form of abl. of *quis*.   **potis** (or *pote*) is the neuter of an old adjec-
tive meaning 'possible'.   8 **bene velle minus**, 'to wish less
well', i.e. 'to be less of a friend'.

34  (LXXV)
1 **huc deducta**, 'brought to such a point'.   2 **officio**, 'devotion'.
4 **omnia**, i.e. everything that is bad.   Ellis compares Shakespeare's

## 35   (LXXXV)

*O what a Heaven is love!   O what a Hell!*
DEKKER

Odi et amo : quare id faciam, fortasse requiris.
nescio, sed fieri sentio et excrucior.


## 36   (LXXIII)   A TREACHEROUS FRIEND

Desine de quoquam quicquam bene velle mereri,
  aut aliquem fieri posse putare pium.
omnia sunt ingrata, nihil fecisse benigne
  prodest, immo etiam taedet obestque magis ;
ut mihi, quem nemo gravius nec acerbius urget,                5
  quam modo qui me unum atque unicum amicum habuit.


## 37   (VIII)

*Shall I, wasting in despair,*
*Die because a woman's fair?*
GEORGE WITHER

Miser Catulle, desinas ineptire,
et quod vides perisse perditum ducas.

Sonnets (LVII) : ' So true a fool is love that in your will, Though
you do anything, he thinks no ill '.

35   (LXXXV)
2 **excrucior,** ' I am in torture '.

36   (LXXIII)
1 **bene mereri** go together : ' to deserve well of '.   2 **pius,** here
' grateful '.   3 **nihil** goes with *prodest* (l. 4).   **fecisse benigne,** 'to
have acted kindly '.   4 **obest,** ' it is harmful '.   5 **ut** (sc. *obest*), here
' so '.   **urget,** ' troubles ', ' vexes '.   6 **modo,** ' just now '.   **unum
atque unicum,** ' one and only '.

37   (VIII)   A soliloquy.   Catullus often addresses poems to him-
self.   In this poem he changes to the third person (l. 12) and back
again to the second (l. 19).
1 **desinas,** subjunctive expressing a mild command : ' You should
cease '.   2 **ducas,** here ' think '.

fulsere quondam candidi tibi soles,
cum ventitabas quo puella ducebat
amata nobis quantum amabitur nulla.                          5
ibi illa multa tum jocosa fiebant,
quae tu volebas nec puella nolebat.
fulsere vere candidi tibi soles.
nunc jam illa non vult : tu quoque impotens noli,
nec quae fugit sectare, nec miser vive,                      10
sed obstinata mente perfer, obdura.
vale, puella.   jam Catullus obdurat,
nec te requiret nec rogabit invitam.
at tu dolebis, cum rogaberis nulla.
scelesta, vae te!   quae tibi manet vita!                    15
quis nunc te adibit?   cui videberis bella?
quem nunc amabis?   cujus esse diceris?
quem basiabis?   cui labella mordebis?
at tu, Catulle, destinatus obdura.

4 **ventito**, frequentative of **venio**.  9 **jam ... non** =*non ...jam*,
'no longer'.  **impotens** can mean either ' headstrong ' or ' power-
less ', here probably the latter.  10 sc. *eam* before **quae**.  **sectare**,
imperative of *sector*, ' pursue '.  11 **obdura**, ' be firm '.  12 addressed
to Lesbia.  14 **nulla**, strong form of *non*, ' not at all ', like our ' not
a bit of you '.  15 **vae te!** ' Woe is thee ! '  The reading is doubtful.
Bury ingeniously conjectures *anenti*, ' (grown) an old woman ', and
reads *scelesta, anenti quae tibi manet vita?*  19 **destinatus**, ' re-
solved ', ' steadfast '.

# CHAPTER V

## A YEAR ABROAD

IF you visit Rome you may see the ruins of a fine villa on the Palatine which has been identified as Clodia's. You climb a steep hill that rises immediately behind the House of the Vestals in the Forum and come to a street, formerly one of the most fashionable in Rome, where the houses of Cicero, Clodius, Caelius Rufus and Clodia formerly stood. Clodia was now a well-to-do widow and here entertained the gay set of Rome. Catullus, bitterly estranged from her and no longer a welcome guest, decided to go abroad for a year, doubtless to forget her. The recent death of his brother gave him another reason for going, as it enabled him to visit his tomb near Troy. At the age of twenty-seven he obtained a post on the staff of Memmius, who had just been elected propraetor of Bithynia (the part of Asia Minor south-east of the Propontis). Memmius was a cultured magistrate and an occasional poet. Lucretius had dedicated his *De Rerum Natura* to him.

It was the custom of young Roman aristocrats to go abroad for colonial experience with a view to a political career. Catullus may have now wanted something more active than writing poetry. In poem 38, which he wrote to a friend, probably from Verona as he passed through, he says he feels his brother's death too deeply to write more poetry. He was also hard-up ; the life of a young man-about-town in the last days of the Republic was expensive. Clodia had doubtless depleted his resources till his ' purse ' was ' full of cobwebs ', as he says in poem 2, though he still possessed country villas at Tivoli and Sirmio.

The members of the governor's suite (*cohors praetoria*) were not given regular salaries, but were expected to enrich themselves through the iniquitous system by which the governor farmed out the tax-gathering in the provinces to joint-stock companies (*societates publicanorum*). These companies would pay the government a lump sum and employ local agents to collect the money. At a later date St. Matthew was thus employed. In addition to this the governor would get pickings for himself and his train. How much an unprincipled governor could extort is revealed by Cicero in his speech against Verres, a governor of Sicily fifteen years before.

We are not told how Catullus spent his year abroad, but he certainly did not come back with the fortune for which he had hoped. In poem 43 he lays the blame on Memmius, ' who gave no thought to his staff ', but how far the abuse that Catullus hurled upon him was deserved we do not know.

It was probably on the outward voyage that he visited his brother's tomb in the Troad and wrote poem 39, the simplicity of which is far more impressive than the lengthier and more elaborate elegies of later poets. It is a farewell of deeper sadness because of its finality, offering no hope of a future reunion.

In the following spring the idea of a Greek cruise stirred him to action. He decided to tour ' the famous cities of Asia Minor ' before he returned home. Farewell Bithynia! *Jam ver egelidos refert tepores!* ' Spring is in the air *now* ' (poem 40) strikes again the note of joy that we have not heard since the first lyrics to Lesbia. Winter is hard in the country south-east of the Propontis, but in spring the region bursts into bloom, flowering shrubs cover the undulating plains, and the sound of waters takes the place of the stillness of winter snows. Horace also wrote two poems on the spring, *Diffugere nives* and *Solvitur acris hiems*, which it is interesting to compare with this poem, but Horace used spring as a peg for a moral, ' Live for to-day, the autumn of life is coming '. Catullus's poem is the expression of spring itself, and the youthful spirit of adventure which spring arouses even in old and hardened travellers.

His homeward journey was made in a yacht called a *phaselus*, because it was shaped like a kidney-bean. He had saved enough money to have it built on the shores of the Black Sea, and sailed for him through the Hellespont along the coast of Asia Minor to Nicaea, where he probably stepped on board. In poem 42 we can follow his course to Rhodes, 'the isle of roses', whose city was renowned in antiquity as the possessor of the Colossus, a huge statue of the Sun-God which ranked as a wonder of the world. Thence he sailed across to the Cyclades, perhaps visiting the little island of Delos in their midst, where Apollo and his twin sister Artemis were born. It was to Artemis, under the name of Diana, that he had written the hymn which is printed here as poem 19. He passed on, over the Isthmus of Corinth—strangely enough there is no mention of Athens—to the Adriatic, even into the river Po itself, and so to Sirmio, his country home on the lovely Lake Garda. There the yacht passed the rest of its days in honourable retirement as one that has, in Masefield's words,

> Heard the song of the blossoms and the old chant of the sea,
> And seen strange lands from under the arched white sails of ships.

Virgil wrote a parody on this poem, which we possess. He was about fourteen when Catullus's yacht passed through Mantua, his home on the river Mincio which flows into Lake Garda. Poem 41 is a greeting to his 'all-but island, olive-silvery Sirmio', an expression of the joy of home-coming which would be difficult to match in Latin literature.

### 38  (LXVIII)  HIS BROTHER'S DEATH

*All my life's bliss from thy dear life was given,*
*All my life's bliss is in the grave with thee.*
EMILY BRONTË

Tempore quo primum vestis mihi tradita pura est,     15
    jucundum cum aetas florida ver ageret,
multa satis lusi : non est dea nescia nostri,
    quae dulcem curis miscet amaritiem :
sed totum hoc studium luctu fraterna mihi mors
    abstulit.   o misero frater adempte mihi,     20
tu mea tu moriens fregisti commoda, frater,
    tecum una tota est nostra sepulta domus,
omnia tecum una perierunt gaudia nostra,
    quae tuus in vita dulcis alebat amor.
cujus ego interitu tota de mente fugavi     25
    haec studia atque omnes delicias animi.

38  (LXVIII)  A portion of a poem to a friend, in which Catullus
says he is too deeply grieved by his brother's death to write more
love poems.
15 **vestis ... pura,** ' white toga ' (*toga virilis*) assumed by the
Roman boy at about sixteen, when he became a man, in place of
the purple-bordered toga of boyhood (*toga praetexta*).  16 **aetas
florida,** ' my youth in its bloom '.  17 **multa satis lusi,** ' I wrote
enough love poems '.  **dea,** i.e. Venus.  **nostri,** ' of me ', plural
for singular.  Cf. *nostra* for *mea* in ll. 22 and 23.  18 **curis,** ' love '.
**amaritiem,** ' bitterness '.  19 **hoc studium,** ' enthusiasm for
this '.  **fraterna mors** = *mors fratris*.  20 **adempte mihi,** ' snatched
away from me ' (lit. ' to my disadvantage ').  21 **fregisti,** ' shat-
tered '.  **commoda,** ' happiness '.  22 **una.**  Scan.  Why can it
not agree with *domus*?  26 **studia,** ' pursuits '.

### 39  (CI)

*Thou'lt come no more,*
*Never, never, never, never, never.*
SHAKESPEARE, *King Lear*

Multas per gentes et multa per aequora vectus
advenio has miseras, frater, ad inferias,

ut te postremo donarem munere mortis
   et mutam nequiquam alloquerer cinerem.
quandoquidem fortuna mihi tete abstulit ipsum,      5
   heu miser indigne frater adempte mihi,
nunc tamen interea haec prisco quae more parentum
   tradita sunt tristi munere ad inferias,
accipe fraterno multum manantia fletu,
   atque in perpetuum, frater, ave atque vale.      10


### 40 (XLVI)

*Just now the lilac is in bloom*
*All before my little room.*
RUPERT BROOKE

Jam ver egelidos refert tepores,
jam caeli furor aequinoctialis
jucundis Zephyri silescit auris.
linquantur Phrygii, Catulle, campi
Nicaeaeque ager uber aestuosae ;      5
ad claras Asiae volemus urbes.

39 (CI) Written after visiting his brother's tomb near Troy, perhaps at the tomb itself. Note the mournful effect of the repeated use of the letter ' m ' in this poem. For a modern translation see page 88.
2 **inferias,** ' honours ' (to the dead), ' obsequies '. 3 **munere mortis,** ' death gift ', wine, milk, honey, etc. 5 **quandoquidem,** ' since '. **tete,** cf. *sese.* **indigne.** The scansion will tell you whether this is vocative or an adverb. 7 **tamen interea,** implying that Catullus intends to return one day to do more—possibly to erect a cenotaph (Ellis). The order is : *accipe haec, quae prisco more parentum* . . . 8 **tristi munere,** ' by way of a sad gift ', i.e. ' as sorrow's tribute '. **ad,** ' for the purpose of '. 9 **manantia,** ' wet ', from **manare,** ' to trickle ', agreeing with *haec* (l. 7). 10 **ave atque vale,** formula of farewell at a funeral.

40 (XLVI) Written on leaving Bithynia in the spring of 56 B.C., to tour ' the renowned cities of Asia Minor ' on his way home.
1 **egelidos,** lit. ' ex-chill ', i.e. ' no longer cold '. 2 **caeli,** ' weather '. **aequinoctialis,** i.e. the equinox at the end of March. 3 **auris,** from *aura,* ' breezes '. 5 **Nicaeae,** capital of Bithynia (v. map, p. 76). **uber,** ' fertile '. 6 **volemus** from *volare,* not *velle.*

jam mens praetrepidans avet vagari,
jam laeti studio pedes vigescunt.
o dulces comitum valete coetus,
longe quos simul a domo profectos                    10
diversae variae viae reportant.

## 41   (XXXI)

*Home is the sailor, home from sea.*
R. L. Stevenson

Paene insularum, Sirmio, insularumque
ocelle, quascumque in liquentibus stagnis
marique vasto fert uterque Neptunus ;
quam te libenter quamque laetus inviso,
vix mi ipse credens Thyniam atque Bithynos            5
liquisse campos et videre te in tuto.
o quid solutis est beatius curis,
cum mens onus reponit, ac peregrino
labore fessi venimus larem ad nostrum,

**7 praetrepidans,** 'fluttering in anticipation'. **avet,** 'longs'.
**comitum,** i.e. the other members of the governor's staff. **coetus,**
'gatherings'. **10 longe.** Take with *a domo profectos.* **11 diversae,**
'in different directions'. **variae,** 'through different lands'.

**41 (XXXI)** Sirmio is a peninsula on the south of Lake Garda in
North Italy, where Catullus had a country house. In this poem he
expresses his joy at seeing it again after his year's absence in
Bithynia. Note the effect of the repeated use of the letter ' l ' in
this poem. Tennyson obtains a similar liquid effect in *Morte
d'Arthur* : ' I heard the water lapping on the crag, And the long
ripple . . . '
**2 ocelle,** ' little eye ' (v. note on 14. 18). The long peninsula
(*paene insula*) jutting out into the oval lake might well suggest this
comparison to a poet. At times the narrow strip of land connecting
Sirmio with the mainland is submerged, and the peninsula looks
like an island. **liquentibus stagnis,** ' clear lakes '. **3 uterque
Neptunus,** ' either water-god ', i.e. god of salt water or fresh
water. **4 inviso,** ' visit '. **5** sc. *me* after **credens** as subject to
*liquisse* (or possibly the Greek use of nominative and infinitive, as
in 42. 2). **8, 9 peregrino labore,** ' toil abroad '. **larem,** ' house-
hold god ' (whose image stood on the hearth), here ' hearth and

Italian State Railways

RUINS OF ROMAN HOUSES ON THE PALATINE, NEAR WHICH CLODIA
HAD A VILLA

*Italian State Railways*

"OLIVE-SILVERY SIRMIO" (poem 41)

desideratoque acquiescimus lecto?    10
hoc est quod unum est pro laboribus tantis.
salve, o venusta Sirmio, atque hero gaude ;
gaudete vosque, o Lydiae lacus undae ;
ridete quidquid est domi cachinnorum.


## 42  (IV)  THE OLD YACHT

Phaselus ille, quem videtis, hospites,
ait fuisse navium celerrimus,

home '.   10 All the joy of homecoming is expressed in this line.
**desiderato, v.** note on *desiderium*, 13. 5.   12 **venusta,** ' charming '.
**hero gaude,** ' rejoice for (i.e. to please) your master '.   13 **gaudete
vosque,** in prose the order would be *vosque gaudete*.  **Lydiae**—a
well-known crux.  It is difficult to discover what word Catullus
wrote.  One MS reads *lidiae*, which is untranslatable, another
*lydiae*.  *Lydiae* can be explained either as Etruscan (**v.** Vergil, *Aen.*
2. 782, *Lydius Thybris*), or as referring to Lydia's golden river, the
Pactolus, which Catullus probably saw on his tour through Asia
Minor, but to describe Lake Garda as ' Lydian ' is unlike Catullus
and contrary to the spirit of the poem, unless perhaps he is still full
of the holiday spirit and cannot help seeing in his home lake the
golden waters he has visited on his tour.  Other editors have sug-
gested *limpidae* (applied to the lake in 42. 24), *lucidae* and *vividae*,
but these are far from the MS.  Scaliger ingeniously suggested
*ludiae*, ' playful '.  *Ludius* is a ' merry man ' or ' tumbler '.  Tyrrel
mentions that some waterfalls in England are still called ' merry
men ' and quotes Stevenson's tale, ' The Merry Men ', named after
a waterfall.  Which reading do you think is right ?   14 Take **quid-
quid cachinnorum** together, ' all the laughs that are at home ',
like *omnibus cachinnis* in 2. 5.

**42   (IV)**   Catullus, now back in his country house at Sirmio, is
showing his guests the old yacht, ' once the fastest of ships ', which
had brought him home from Bithynia.  He traces its course back-
wards to Amastris on the Black Sea, where it was built.  It was
probably carried across the Isthmus of Corinth and towed up the
Po, but how it got up the Mincio into Lake Garda is a problem.
**1 phaselus,** a Greek word ($\phi\acute{\alpha}\sigma\eta\lambda os$) meaning ' a kidney bean ', hence
' yacht ' because shaped like one.  **hospites,** ' guests ', ' friends '.
**2 ait fuisse . . . celerrimus** =*ait se fuisse celerrimum*, an imitation
of the Greek nominative and infinitive construction, cf. 41. 5.

neque ullius natantis impetum trabis
nequisse praeterire, sive palmulis
opus foret volare sive linteo.                    5
et hoc negat minacis Adriatici
negare litus insulasve Cycladas

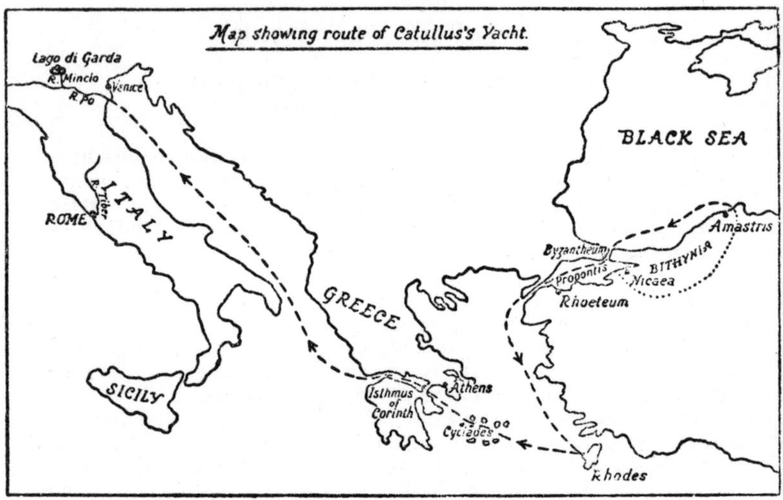



Rhodumque nobilem horridamque Thraciam
Propontida, trucemve Ponticum sinum,
ubi iste post phaselus antea fuit            10

3 **natantis,** ' afloat '.  **impetum** ... **praeterire,** ' exceed the
speed '.  **trabis** (from *trabs*), ' timber '.  4 **palmulis,** ' oars '.
5 **foret** = *esset.*   6 **hoc negat ... negare,** *hoc* is object of
*negare,* ' the yacht says that this is not denied by ...'  7 **Cycladas,**
Greek accus. pl.  A group of islands round Delos in the Aegean.
8 **nobilem,** ' famous ' for its university, its remarkable statue, the
Colossus, and the skill of its inhabitants in navigation.  **horridam,**
' bleak ', lit. ' bristly '.  **Thraciam,** adjective agreeing with *Pro-*
*pontida.*  9 **Propontida,** Greek accus. sing. of *Propontis,* Sea of
Marmora.  10 **iste post phaselus,** ' she, afterwards a yacht '—

comata silva : nam Cytorio in jugo
loquente saepe sibilum edidit coma.
Amastri Pontica et Cytore buxifer,
tibi haec fuisse et esse cognitissima
ait phaselus : ultima ex origine                    15
tuo stetisse dicit in cacumine,
tuo imbuisse palmulas in aequore,
et inde tot per impotentia freta
herum tulisse, laeva sive dextera
vocaret aura, sive utrumque Juppiter                20
simul secundus incidisset in pedem.
neque ulla vota litoralibus deis
sibi esse facta, cum veniret a mari
novissimo hunc ad usque limpidum lacum.
sed haec prius fuere : nunc recondita               25
senet quiete seque dedicat tibi,
gemelle Castor et gemelle Castoris.[1]

an adverb qualifying a noun, common in Greek but rare in Latin.
11 **comata**, ' leafy '.  **Cytorio**, ' of Cytorus ', a mountain near
Amastris (l. 13) and covered with ' boxwood ' (*buxifer*).  12 **lo-
quente coma**, ' when the leaves rustled '.  13 **Amastri**, Greek
voc. of *Amastris*, a port on the Black Sea, facing Mt. Cytorus.
Catullus now turns to address both places, but uses the singular
*tibi*.  14 **cognitissima**.  Notice the unusual superlative of a par-
ticiple.  15 **ultima ex origine**, ' from her very birth '.  17 **im-
buisse**, ' dipped ', i.e. for the first time.  18 **impotentia**, ' raging ',
lit. ' without control '.  19 **laeva ... dextera**, sc. another *sive*
before *laeva*, ' tacking right or left, or running straight before a
favourable wind ' (*Juppiter secundus*).  21 **pedem**, ' sail ', lit. the
sheet (rope) attached to the sail, for setting it to the wind.  22 **lito-
ralibus deis**, ' gods of the sea-shore ', to whom no votive offerings
were made on safe arrival because the yacht was never in danger.
Modern Greeks still dedicate as *vota* little silver models of ships in
the Church of St. Mary in Tinos, one of the Cyclades.  24 **novis-
simo**, ' furthest '.  **ad usque**, ' right up to '.  25 **recondita**,
' secluded '.  26 **senet**, ' spends her old age ', from *seneo*, ' am
old ', an archaic word.  27 **gemelle**. Castor and his ' twin '
brother Pollux were the protectors of sailors (v. Acts xxviii. 11).

[1] For Virgil's witty parody of this poem, see page 96.

## 43 (x)  A BLUFF CALLED

*And Venus to the Loves around*
*Remark'd, how ill we all dissembled.*

MATTHEW PRIOR

Varus me meus ad suos amores
visum duxerat e foro otiosum,
scortillum, ut mihi tum repente visum est,
non sane illepidum neque invenustum.
huc ut venimus, incidere nobis                    5
sermones varii, in quibus, quid esset
jam Bithynia, quo modo se haberet,
et quonam mihi profuisset aere.
respondi, id quod erat, nihil neque ipsis
nec praetoribus esse nec cohorti,               10
cur quisquam caput unctius referret,
praesertim quibus esset irrumator
praetor, non faceret pili cohortem.
' at certe tamen ', inquiunt, ' quod illic
natum dicitur esse, comparasti                  15
ad lecticam homines.'  Ego, ut puellae
unum me facerem beatiorem,

43 (x) Catullus visits Varus after his return from Bithynia, where he had not made the fortune he had expected, and tells a story against himself of how he was shown up bluffing about having brought back ' eight strapping fellows ' to carry his litter.
1 **suos amores,** ' his girl friend '. 2 **visum,** not past participle. Parse. **otiosum,** ' as I was idling '. 3 **scortillum,** ' a little minx '. **repente,** ' at first sight '. 4 ' not entirely unattractive or lacking in the appeal of her sex '. 5 **incidere** = *inciderunt.* 6-7 **quid esset jam Bithynia,** ' what was Bithynia like nowadays '. 8 **quonam ... aere,** ' how much I had got out of it '. 9 **ipsis,** i.e. the natives of the province. 10 **cohorti,** i.e. the staff. 11 **cur ... referret,** an indirect question, ' was there any reason why...' **unctius,** ' better oiled ', i.e. more prosperous. 12-13 ' especially when they had such a swine for a governor, who did not care a straw (*pilus*) for his staff '. 14 **certe,** ' no doubt '. 15 **natum,** ' originated '. **comparasti,** contracted form of *comparavisti,* ' obtained '. 16 **lecticam,** ' litter ' borne by eight men, first used in Bithynia. 17 **unum ... beatiorem,** ' especially lucky '.

' non ', inquam, ' mihi tam fuit maligne,
ut, provincia quod mala incidisset,
non possem octo homines parare rectos.'      20
at mi nullus erat neque hic neque illic,
fractum qui veteris pedem grabati
in collo sibi collocare posset.
hic illa, ut decuit cinaediorem,
' quaeso ', inquit, ' mihi, mi Catulle, paulum      25
istos commoda : nam volo ad Serapim
deferri.'   ' mane ', inquii puellae,
' istud quod modo dixeram me habere,
fugit me ratio : meus sodalis
Cinna est Gaius, is sibi paravit.      30
verum, utrum illius an mei, quid ad me?
utor tam bene quam mihi pararim.
sed tu insulsa male et molesta vivis,
per quam non licet esse neglegentem.'

**18 non mihi tam fuit maligne,** ' I was not so hard up '.   **20 rectos,** ' straight-backed '.   **21 hic,** ' here in Rome ' ; **illic,** ' there in Bithynia '.   **22 grabati,** ' couch '.   **24 ut decuit cinaediorem,** ' like the impudent girl she was '.   **25 quaeso,** colloquial form of *quaero*.   **26 commoda,** ' lend ', imperative. The reading is doubtful (also *mane* next line), as the metre requires a short final syllable in both cases, but cf. *cave* in 9. 18.   **ad Serapim,** ' to the temple of Serapis ', an Egyptian god to whose temple people went for cures.   **27 mane,** ' stop! '   **28 me habere,** a noun clause explaining *istud*, ' as regards what I said just now, that I had them .' **29 fugit me ratio,** ' I made a mistake '.   **30 Cinna est Gaius** ' Cinna—that is Gaius Cinna'. Scan *Gāĭŭs*.   **31 quid ad me?** ' it's all the same to me '.   **32 quam pararim,** for *quam si paraverim*.   **33 insulsa male,** ' very stupid '.   **vivis,** practically = *es*. **34** ' not to let me make a slip of the tongue '.

# CHAPTER VI

## LESBIA—DISILLUSIONMENT

THERE is little more left to say concerning Catullus and
Clodia. The love-affair which had begun so happily dragged
into a series of miserable quarrels. During Catullus's
absence abroad, the fickle Clodia had transferred her affec-
tions to the handsome, clever, young Caelius Rufus, the
friend of Catullus.

But this new attachment was also fated to be brief.
Caelius quarrelled with Clodia, and she, in revenge, started
proceedings against him on a trumped-up charge of attempted
poisoning. Caelius persuaded Cicero to defend him, and it
is from Cicero's speech *Pro Caelio*, delivered in the spring
of 56 B.C., while Catullus was in the East, that we learn
much about Clodia. Cicero exposes the shallowness of the
accusation, and gives a lively picture of the ' banquets, baths,
picnics, pleasure-boats ', and all the extravagant debaucheries
at Rome and Naples with which Clodia amused herself at
this time. Once again, however, we know nothing of
Clodia's argument in defence. As a result of Cicero's
advocacy, Caelius was acquitted, and Clodia's only reward
was the contemptuous nickname of *quadrantaria*, ' the two-
penny halfpenny slut ', and the loss of what little reputation
was left her.

We hear nothing of Catullus's relations with Clodia after
his return from abroad, or even whether he saw her at all,
but if any infatuation remained, these disclosures must
finally have destroyed it. The poem *Siqua recordanti* (no.
44), though its date is uncertain, reveals that he could not
forget her. In verses which are a marvel of compactness

**and** self-revelation he betrays the conflict which still **rages** within him, and prays for delivery and peace of mind.

> Gods, from this festering wound give me release,
> If I have ever served you, grant me peace.

'There is no more passionate poem in the world,' says Maurice Baring.

We are not told how Catullus finally parted from Clodia. Two years later Caesar dined at his father's house in Verona after his invasion of Britain. With characteristic magnanimity he forgave Catullus his satirical epigrams of past days. As a result of this he assumed a fresh importance in Clodia's eyes and she attempted a reconciliation.

Catullus was not to be recaptured. In poem 45 he sends a last message by the hands of the two minions, Furius and Aurelius, who had come with overtures from her. He deliberately wrote it in the Sapphic metre which he had used once before in his first love-letter. Embittered and disillusioned, he imparts a stinging insult in this final repudiation. With pity only for himself in his many sufferings, he declares that Clodia may now live as she chooses, taking to herself three hundred lovers if she please and breaking the hearts of them all. He himself will no longer be her willing plaything. She has crushed his love as if it were a flower on the meadow's edge cut down by the passing plough—she, that ' Lesbia ', whom he loved more than himself and all his friends,

> illa Lesbia, quam Catullus unam
> plus quam se atque suos amavit omnes.

We have a few more lines (poem 46) written, apparently, from a bed of sickness, pleading with Cornificius, a young fellow-poet, to send him a word of consolation. With this our knowledge ends. Catullus died a year or so after, at the age of thirty. Clodia outlived him, and in a letter to Atticus some years later, Cicero asks for news of her.

## 44  (LXXVI)

*Desiring nought but how to kill desire.*
SIR PHILIP SIDNEY

Siqua recordanti benefacta priora voluptas
  est homini, cum se cogitat esse pium,
nec sanctam violasse fidem, nec foedere in ullo
  divum ad fallendos numine abusum homines,
multa parata manent in longa aetate, Catulle,                5
  ex hoc ingrato gaudia amore tibi.
nam quaecumque homines bene cuiquam aut dicere pos-
      sunt
  aut facere, haec a te dictaque factaque sunt ;
omnia quae ingratae perierunt credita menti.
  qua re jam te cur amplius excrucies?                10
quin tu animum offirmas atque istinc te ipse reducis,
  et dis invitis desinis esse miser?
difficile est longum subito deponere amorem.
  difficile est, verum hoc qualibet efficias :
una salus haec est, hoc est tibi pervincendum,                15
  hoc facias, sive id non pote sive pote.
o di, si vestrum est misereri, aut si quibus umquam
  extremam jam ipsa in morte tulistis opem,
me miserum aspicite et, si vitam puriter egi,
  eripite hanc pestem perniciemque mihi ;                20

44  (LXXVI)
1 Siqua, ' if any ', agreeing with *voluptas*. **recordanti** from
*recordor*, ' call to mind ', ' recollect '. 2 **pium**, ' loyal ', ' one
who does his duty '. This word is the basis of Roman morals and
expresses duty to gods, city and family. 4 **divum**, for *deorum*.
**abusum**, from *abutor*, ' abuse the sanctity of the gods '. 5-6 The
order is : *multa gaudia tibi parata manent in longa aetate* (life) *ex hoc
ingrato amore*. 7 Take **bene** with *dicere* and *facere*. 9 **omnia
quae** =*quae omnia*, ' all this love, given to an ungrateful heart, has
been wasted '. **menti**, i.e. of Lesbia. 11 **quin**, ' why not ? '
(its original meaning). **istinc**, i.e. from the love. 14 **verum
qualibet**, ' but in any way you can '. 16 **pote**, neuter of *potis*,
' possible '. sc. ' *est fieri* '.

heu, mihi surrepens imos ut torpor in artus
   expulit ex omni pectore laetitias!
non jam illud quaero, contra ut me diligat illa,
   aut, quod non potis est, esse pudica velit :
ipse valere opto et taetrum hunc deponere morbum.    25
   o di, reddite mi hoc pro pietate mea.

### 45  (xi)  LAST MESSAGE TO LESBIA

*I can let thee now alone*
*As worthy to be loved by none.*
Sir Robert Ayton

Furi et Aureli, comites Catulli,
sive in extremos penetrabit Indos,
litus ut longe resonante Eoa
   tunditur unda,

sive in Hyrcanos Arabesque molles,    5
seu Sacas sagittiferosve Parthos,
sive quae septemgeminus colorat
   aequora Nilus,

sive trans altas gradietur Alpes,
Caesaris visens monimenta magni,    10
Gallicum Rhenum  horribile aequor, ulti-
   mosque Britannos,

**21 surrepens,** 'creeping stealthily'. **ut,** 'how'. **torpor,** 'lethargy'.
**23 contra,** 'in return'. **24 pudica,** 'chaste', 'faithful'. **25
taetrum,** 'loathsome'.

**45** (**xi**) The reference to Caesar in Britain (10-12) dates this
poem as not earlier than 55 B.C., the year before Catullus's death.
**3 ut,** 'where', a rare use ; also in 28. 10. **Eoa,** 'belonging to the
dawn ' (*Eos*), hence ' eastern '. **5 Hyrcanos,** a people living south
of the Caspian Sea. **molles,** ' soft ' (through oriental luxury).
**6 Sacas,** a tribe of Scythians, living north of the Black Sea. **Parthos,**
also of Scythian race. The Parthians were famous for their skill
in archery. **7 septemgeminus,** the seven mouths of the Nile,
whose muddy waters discolour land and sea. **9 gradietur,** 'march '
**10 monimenta,** i.e. records of Caesar's successes. **11 Rhenum,**
the Rhine, which Caesar was the first Roman to cross. **horribile**

omnia haec, quaecumque feret voluntas
caelitum, temptare simul parati,
pauca nuntiate meae puellae     15
    non bona dicta.

cum suis vivat valeatque moechis,
quos simul complexa tenet trecentos,
nullum amans vere, sed identidem omnium
    ilia rumpens :     20

nec meum respectet, ut ante, amorem,
qui illius culpa cecidit velut prati
ultimi flos, praetereunte postquam
    tactus aratro est.

## 46  (XXXVIII)

## TO CORNIFICIUS—WRITTEN IN SICKNESS

*Prithee, a little talk for ease*
*Full as the tears of old Simonides.*
            LEIGH HUNT

Male est, Cornifici, tuo Catullo,
male est, me hercule! et laboriose,
et magis magis in dies et horas.

**aequor.** The MS. has *horribilesque*, 'savage', a more fitting
epithet for the Britons than the sea, but involving an awkward
metrical hiatus. Another reading is *horribilem insulam*. **ultimos,**
'at the world's end'. 14 **caelitum,** genitive of *caelites*, 'dwellers
in heavens ', i.e. gods. 15 **meae puellae,** an ironical repetition
of the phrase Catullus had used in the two pet bird poems (13.1
and 14.3). 16 **non bona,** 'unkind'. 17 **moechis,** 'lovers'.
19 **identidem,** the unusual word which Catullus had used in his
first love poem to Lesbia (12.3). He deliberately repeats it in a very
different connection in this last poem of renunciation, and also
employs the same (Sapphic) metre. 20 **ilia rumpens,** 'breaking
the hearts of'. 22-3 **prati ultimi,** 'edge of the meadow'.

46  (XXXVIII)
1. **Cornifici.** Cornificius was a poet and friend of Catullus. **male
est,** 'your Catullus is not well'. This poem may have been

> quem tu, quod minimum facillimumque est,
> qua solatus es allocutione? 5
> irascor tibi.   sic meos amores?
> paulum quidlibet allocutionis,
> maestius lacrimis Simonideis.

written just before Catullus's death.   **6 sic meos amores?**   The verb must be supplied, and *meos amores* is ambiguous.   Either (1) 'Is that how you treat your friend?' or (2) 'Is that how you treat the story of my love?' alluding, perhaps, to some confidence about Lesbia.   **7 paulum quidlibet**, 'just a little word'.   sc. *da.* **8 Simonideis.**   Simonides was a Greek poet of Ceos, famed for his elegies and epitaphs, and in particular the epitaph on the Spartans who died at Thermopylae.

> ὦ ξεῖν', ἀγγέλλειν Λακεδαιμονίοις ὅτι τῇδε
> κείμεθα, τοῖς κείνων ῥήμασι πειθόμενοι·

> Tell them at Lacedaemon, passer-by,
> That here, obedient to their laws, we lie.

# APPENDIX I

## TRANSLATIONS

### 12 (LI)

Φαίνεταί μοι κῆνος ἴσος θέοισιν
ἔμμεν' ὤνηρ, ὄστις ἐνάντιός τοι
ἰζάνει καὶ πλάσιον ἆδυ φωνεί-
    σας ὑπακούει

καὶ γελαίσας ἰμμέροεν· τό μοι μὰν
καρδίαν ἐν στήθεσιν ἐπτόασεν·
ὤς σε γὰρ Ϝίδω βρόχε', ὤς με φώνας
    οὐδὲν ἔτ' εἴκει·

ἀλλὰ κὰμ μὲν γλῶσσα Ϝέαγε, λέπτον δ'
αὔτικα χρῶ πῦρ ὑπαδεδρόμακεν,
ὀππάτεσσι δ' οὐδὲν ὄρημ', ἐπιρρόμ-
    βουσι δ' ἄκουαι·

ἀ δέ μ' ἴδρως κακχέεται, τρόμος δὲ
παῖσαν ἄγρει, χλωροτέρα δὲ ποίας
ἔμμι, τεθνάκην δ' ὀλίγω 'πιδεύης
    φαίνομαι . . .

SAPPHO

Him I hold as happy as God in Heaven,
Who can sit and gaze on your face before him,
Who can sit and hear from your lips that sweetest
    Music you utter—

Hear your lovely laughter, that sets a-tremble
All my heart with flutterings wild as terror.
Ah, when I behold you an instant, straightway
    All my words fail me,

86

Helpless halts my tongue, a devouring fever
Runs like fire through every vein within me,
Darkness veils my vision, my ears are deafened,
    Beating like hammers ;

Cold the sweat runs down me ; a sudden trembling
Leaves my limbs a-quiver ; my face grows paler
Than the summer-grasses ; I see beside me
    Death stand, and madness.

F. L. LUCAS

## 15, 16   (V, VII)

Kiss me, sweet : the wary lover
Can your favours keep, and cover,
When the common courting jay
All your bounties will betray.
Kiss again!  no creature comes ;
Kiss, and score up wealthy sums
On my lips, thus hardly sundered,
While you breathe.  First give a hundred,
Then a thousand, then another
Hundred, then unto the tother
Add a thousand and so more,
Till you equal with the store
All the grass that Rumney yields,
Or the sands in Chelsea fields,
Or the drops in silver Thames,
Or the stars that gild his streams
In the silent summer nights
When Youth plies its stolen delights :
That the curious may not know
How to tell 'em as they flow,
And the envious, when they find
What their number is, be pined.

BEN JONSON<br>(an adaptation of poems 15 and 16)

## 22   (XLV)

Septimius, clasping to his breast
His Acme, cried ' Dear, I protest,

Unless I love to desperation
My Acme—and without cessation
Will love her still, as desperately
As ever woman loved could be,
In Libya's sand or India's heat
May a green-eyed lion your lover meet! "
Soon as he said it, Love well pleased,
As before on the left, on the right hand sneezed.
But Acme, leaning back her head,
With her mouth of cherry-red
Kissed her sweet love's swimming eyes.
' Septimillus, love ', she cries,
' So may we keep the faith we plight
To Love our Lord, as the flame alight
Within this loving heart of mine
Is fiercer and hotter yet than thine! '
Soon as she said it, Love well pleased,
As before on the left, on the right hand sneezed.
So with fortune's fondest blessing
They love alike, possessed, possessing.
For Britain and the East as well
Foolish Septimius would not sell
His Acme.   In Septimius' sight
Is faithful Acme's one delight.
Who ever saw such happiness,
Or hearts that Love so loved to bless?

F. L. LUCAS

## 39 (CI)

Through many seas, my brother, and many a nation
   To this thy bitter burial I come,
Bringing thy death its debt of lamentation,
   My last vain call to thee whose dust is dumb.
Now, since a callous fortune has bereft us
   Each of the other, dear, unhappy head,
By that old custom that our fathers left us
   For the last mournful duties to the dead,
Wet with my weeping take these gifts of me :
Hail, brother, and Farewell—eternally!

F. L. LUCAS

### 41 (XXXI)

Gem of all isthmuses and isles that lie,
Fresh or salt water's children, in clear lake
Or ampler ocean, with what joy do I
Approach thee, Sirmio, Oh!   Am I awake,
Or dream that once again my eye beholds
Thee, and has looked its last on Thynian wolds?
Sweetest of sweets to me that pastime seems,
When the mind drops her burden : when—the pain
Of travel past—our own cot we regain
And nestle on the pillow of our dreams!
'Tis this one thought that cheers us as we roam.
Hail, O fair Sirmio!   Joy, thy lord is here!
Joy too, ye waters of the Garda Mere!
And ring out, all ye laughter-peals of home.

C. S. CALVERLEY

### 42 (IV)

Proud is Phaselus here, my friends, to tell
That once she was the swiftest craft afloat :
No vessel, were she winged with blade or sail,
Could ever pass my boat.
Phaselus shunned to shun grim Adria's shore,
Or Cyclades, or Rhodes the wide renowned,
Or Bosphorus, where Thracian waters roar,
Or Pontus' eddying sound.
It was in Pontus once, unwrought, she stood,
And conversed, sighing, with her sister trees,
Amastris born, or where Cytorus' wood
Answers the mountain breeze.
Pontic Amastris, boxwood-clad Cytorus!—
You, says Phaselus, are her closest kin :
Yours were the forests where she stood inglorious :
The waters yours wherein
She dipped her virgin blades ;  and from your strand
She bore her master through the cringing straits,
Nought caring were the wind on either hand,
Or whether kindly fates
Filled both the straining sheets.   Never a prayer

For her was offered to the gods of haven,
Till last she left the sea, hither to fare,
And to be lightly laven
By the cool ripple of the clear lagoon.

This too is past ; at length she is allowed
Long slumber through her  life's long afternoon,
To Castor and the twin of Castor vowed.

JAMES ELROY FLECKER

### 44   (LXXVI)

If it can please a man to recollect
His deeds of kindness done, and to reflect
That he has shown true loyalty in act
And word unto his friends, nor in a pact
Misused the gods to cheat his fellow men,
Your unrequited love should earn you then,
Catullus, life-long joys in overflow ;
For what of kindness man to man may show,
In word or deed was said and done by you :
All this was given to a heart untrue :
And it is lost : then wherefore, spirit-sore,
Torment yourself with anguish any more?
Nay, stand entrenched within your peace to be,
And doff, despite the gods, your misery.
'Tis hard to bid long-rooted love begone,
But must in this way or in that be done.
There alone safety lies!   This, carry through :
This, if you can or cannot, you must do.
Ye gods, if mercy lives within your span,
If you have ever helped a dying man,
Look down upon me in my agony ;
My life was clean, so take this plague from me.
Ah me!  within my inmost bones a blight
Has crept, and in my heart killed all delight.
I ask no more that she be kind to me—
Nor become chaste, for that could never be ;
Gods, from this festering wound give me release,
If I have ever served you, grant me peace.

MAURICE BARING

# APPENDIX II

## THE METRES OF CATULLUS

Catullus, like other poets, employed a variety of metres for his poems, according to what he wished to express. He used several Greek metres, some of which he was the first Roman poet to employ. Horace and Martial followed this practice, adopting a stricter form, in contrast to the freedom which Catullus, like his Greek models, frequently allowed himself. His favourite metre was the hendecasyllabic.

I *Hendecasyllables* (from the Greek ἔνδεκα, eleven).
*Poems* 1, 2, 3, 4, 5, 8, 9, 13, 14, 15, 16, 20, 22, 26, 40, 43, 46.

*Scheme.*

e.g.

| 'Look, I | come to the | test, a | tiny | po-em |
| All com- | posed in a | me-tre | of Ca- | tullus '. |
| Pass - er, | del - ic - i- | ae me- | ae pu- | ellae |

(poem 13)

There is usually a caesura, or pause, after the fifth or sixth syllable.

Occasionally a monosyllable at the end of the line gives a striking effect, e.g. :

> brevis lux (15.5)
> tacet nox (16.7)

Catullus had such mastery over this metre that he used it with equal success for a dedication, a spring song, an invitation to dinner, scurrilous lampoons and passionate love poems. Tennyson imitated it in his poem

'O you chorus of indolent reviewers'.

II *Elegiacs*—two lines, a *hexameter* (6 feet), followed by a *pentameter* (5 feet made up of twice 2½ feet).

Poems 6, 10, 11, 17, 18, 23, 30, 31, 32, 33, 34, 35, 36, 38, 39, 44.

*Scheme of hexameter.*

|  —  ◡ ◡ | — ◡ ◡ | — ◡ ◡ | — ◡ ◡ | — ◡ ◡ | — ◡ |
| --- | --- | --- | --- | --- | --- |
| e.g.   Down in a | deep dark | dell sat an | old sow | chewin' a | bean-stalk. |
| Si-qua re- | cor - dan- | ti   bene- | facta pri- | ora  vol- | uptas |

(poem 44)

*Scheme of pentameter.*

| — ◡ ◡ | — ◡ ◡ | — ‖ — ◡ ◡ | — ◡ ◡ | ◡ |
| --- | --- | --- | --- | --- |
| e.g.   Out of her | mouth came | forth, ‖ grunts of a | greedy del- | ight. |
| Atqu(e) in | perpetu- | um, ‖ frater av(e) | atque  val- | e. |

(poem 39)

Unlike Ovid, Catullus frequently ended pentameters with words of three or more syllables, e.g. :

> surripuit Veneres (17.6)
> Hortale, virginibus (11.2)
> flemus amicitias (10.4)

and, in a poem not in this selection, even with a word of seven syllables,

> Audit falsiparens Amphitryoniades.

He used elision freely, even at times harshly, e.g.

Quant(a) in am- | ore tu(o) | ex ‖ parte rep- | erta me (a) | est (18.4)
Quam modo qui m(e) un(um) atqu(e) unic(um) amic(um) habuit.

(36.6)

He allowed, again like the Greek poets, the sentences to run on from one couplet to another, as in poem 39.

III *Hexameters*—scheme as above.
Poem 24.

Catullus allowed himself licences usually avoided by later poets, e.g. a spondee in the fifth foot, as pervincendum (44.15), agitur decursu (11.23).

IV *Sapphics.*
*Poems* 7, 12, 45.
*Scheme* (first three lines).

|  –  ‿ | –  – | –  ‿  ‿ | –  ‿ | –  ‿ |
|---|---|---|---|---|
| e.g.  Needy | knife grin- | der !  Whither | are   you | going ? |
| Līt-ŭs | ūt   lŏn | ge   rĕs-ŏn- | ant-(e) Ĕ- | ō ā |

*Scheme* (fourth line).

|  –  ‿  ‿ | –  – |
|---|---|
| e.g.                          Scissors to | grind Ō ! |
| Tundit-ur | und-a. |

Catullus sometimes imitates Sappho's metre more closely than Horace, e.g.

(1) in the use of a trochee (– ‿) in the second foot, as

        seu Sac- | ās săg- | ittiferosve Parthos (45.6)

        pauca | nūntĭ- | ate meae puellae (45.15)

(2) in the absence of caesura, as

        sive quae septemgeminus colorat (45.7).

(3) in an occasional elision at the end of a line before a vowel in
    the following line, as

                omnium (45.19).

V *Iambics* (trimeter)—six iambic (‿ –) feet.
*Poem* 42.
*Scheme.*

| ‿  – | ‿  – | ‿  – | ‿  – | ‿  – | ‿  – |
|---|---|---|---|---|---|
| e.g.  'The pún- | y pín- | nace yón- | der you, | my friends, | discérn' |
| Phas - el - | us il- | le,  quem | vid - e - | tis,   hosp- | it-es |

                          (poem 42)

Poem 42 is written in pure iambic metre, without a single
spondee, a remarkable achievement in the Latin language, which
has an excess of long syllables.  Catullus was deliberately trying
to give the effect of his yacht lightly speeding over the sea.

VI. *Scazon or ' limping ' Iambics*—five iambic feet followed by
a spondee (– –).
*Poems* 21, 25, 27, 37, 41.
*Scheme.*

e.g.    'Egnat- | i - us, | the || own- | er  of | superb | white teeth'
        O fun- | de nos- | ter || seu | Sa-bi- | ne  seu | Ti-burs

(poem 21)

This metre is similar to the iambic except that the last foot
is a spondee, which slows up the end of the line with a jolt.
Meredith frequently uses the same device, a kind of hammerbeat,
e.g. ' Wavy in the dusk lit by one large star ' (*Love in a Valley*).
There is usually a caesura in the third foot.

Catullus employs the metre with equal success for his lyric
rapture on returning to his lake-side home, *Paene insularum
Sirmio*, and for the agonising soliloquy, *Miser Catulle*.

VII *Miscellaneous metres containing Glyconics and Pherecrateans.*
*Poems* 19, 28, 29.

A *Glyconic* scans

e.g.    'Queen and | Empress of | India,
        Crowned so | long with a | diadem
        Nev  -  er | worn  by  a | worthier '

(from Tennyson's *Ode on the Jubilee of Queen Victoria*).

A *Pherecratean* (invented by Pherecrates, an Athenian comic
poet) scans

e.g.    'Swiftly | over the | water'

*Poem* 28—a Glyconic plus a Pherecratean :

e.g.

'Headlong | into the | mire below || topsy- | turvy to | drown him '.
(ELLIS).

O      col- | on -i-a, | quae cupis || ponte | luder -e | longo.

*Poem* 19—Three Glyconic lines followed by a Pherecratean :

$$\text{Dĭ-ā- } | \text{ nām pŭ-ĕ- } | \text{ r(ī) intĕgrī (Glyconic)}$$

$$\text{Pŭ-e-ll- } | \text{ āequĕ că- } | \text{ nāmŭs (Pherecratean)}$$

*Poem* 29—Four Glyconic lines followed by a Pherecratean :

$$\text{Hūc vĕ- } | \text{ nī, nĭvĕ- } | \text{ ō gĕrēns (Glyconic)}$$

$$\text{lūtĕ- } | \text{ ūm pĕdĕ } | \text{ sōccūm (Pherecratean)}$$

# APPENDIX III

## LINES FROM VERGIL'S PARODY OF POEM 42 (IV) "THE OLD YACHT" (PHASELUS ILLE)

Vergil when a boy may have seen Catullus' yacht towed up the Mincio past his home.  In this parody, which is probably by Vergil, though it is not certain, instead of the speedy yacht returning from Asia Minor we have Sabinus and his mules plodding their way through the muddy lanes of Cisalpine Gaul. Sabinus, whoever he was, is pictured as dedicating on his retirement a votive offering to Castor and Pollux, in gratitude for being saved from the dangers of the highways.  The offering was a representation of himself sitting like an officer-of-state in a curule chair.

> Sabinus ille, quem videtis, hospites,
> ait fuisse mulio [1] celerrimus
> neque ullius volantis impetum cisi [2]
> nequisse praeterire, sive Mantuam
> opus foret volare sive Brixiam.
>
> .     .     .     .     .     .
>
> Cremona frigida et lutosa [3] Gallia,
> tibi haec fuisse et esse cognitissima
> ait Sabinus : ultima ex origine
> tua stetisse dicit in voragine,

[1] ' muleteer '.

[2] gen. of *cisium* ' two-wheeled carriage, gig '.  *impetum* here ' speed '.

[3] ' muddy '.

tua in palude deposisse sarcinas, [1]
et inde tot per orbitosa milia [2]
iugum tulisse, laeva [3] sive dextera
strigare mula sive utrimque coeperat

.    .    .    .    .

neque ulla vota semitalibus [4] deis
sibi [5] esse facta, praeter hoc novissimum,
paterna lora proximumque pectinem [6]
sed haec prius fuere : nunc eburnea [7]
sedetque sede seque dedicat tibi,
gemelle Castor et gemelle Castoris. [8]

[1] ' pack '. *deposisse* for *deposuisse*.

[2] ' miles full of cart-ruts '. *orbita* ' a cart-track '

[3] ' whether the mule on the left or on the right or on both sides began to tire '. *strigare* ' to halt in ploughing ', and so ' flag '.

[4] ' of the lanes ' (*semita*). Statues of gods were often placed in by-ways. Cf. Trivia (poem 19), who was worshipped at cross-roads.

[5] ' by himself ' for *a se*.

[6] ' comb '.          [7] ' of ivory '.

[8] ' Castor's twin-brother ', i.e. Pollux.

# VOCABULARY

*(N.B.—The hyphens indicate, not a natural break in the word, but the letters from the nominative or the present stem which are to be repeated.)*

## A

**ā, ab,** *prep. with abl.,* from, by.

**ab-eo, -īre, -ii, -itum,** 4, go away, depart.

**abhorr-eo, -ēre, -ui, —,** 2, recoil from, differ from.

**abitus,** 4 *m.,* departure, exit, outlet.

**abscond-o, -ere, -i, -itum,** 3, hide, conceal.

**abstuli,** *see* **aufero.**

**absūm-o, -ere, -psi, -ptum,** 3, use up, destroy.

**abūt-or, -i, abūsus sum,** 3 *dep.,* use up, abuse *(with abl.).*

**ac,** *see* **atque.**

**accid-o, -ere, -i, —,** 3, reach, happen, result.

**acc-ipio, -ipere, -ēpi, -eptum,** 3, receive. **acceptus,** acceptable, welcome.

**accub-o, -are, -ui, -itum,** 1, lie at, recline.

**āc-er, -ris, -re,** *adj.,* keen.

**acerbē,** *adv.,* grievously.

**acervus,** 2 *m.,* heap.

**Achill-ēs, -is,** 3 *m.,* Achilles, a Greek hero.

**Achīvus,** *adj.,* Greek.

**Acm-ē, -ēs,** 3 *f.,* Acme, lover of Septimius, friend of Catullus.

**acqui-esco, -escere, -ēvi, -ētum,** 3, repose, find rest.

**acūtus,** *adj.,* pointed, sharp, shrill.

**ad,** *prep. with acc.,* to, towards.

**ad-eo, -īre, -ii, -itum,** 4, go to, approach.

**adeptus,** *see* **adipiscor.**

**ad-imo, -imere, -ēmi, -emptum,** 3, deprive, snatch away.

**adipisc-or, -i, adeptus sum,** 3 *dep.,* attain to, reach.

**aditus,** 4 *m.,* approach, access.

**ad-lūdo, -lūdere, -lūsi, -lūsum,** 3, play with.

**admīror,** 1 *dep.,* wonder at, admire.

**adpet-o, -ere, -īvi, -ītum,** 3, strive after, peck.

**Adriāticum,** 2 *n.,* the Adriatic sea.

**ad-sum, -esse, -fui,** be present.

**ad-venio, -venīre, -vēni, -ventum,** 4, arrive.

**adventus,** 4 *m.,* arrival.

**adversus,** *prep. with acc.,* opposite, facing.

**aequē,** *adv.,* equally.

**aequinoctiāl-is, -e,** *adj.,* of the equinox, equinoctial.

**aequo,** 1, make smooth.

**aequ-or, -oris,** 3 *n.,* a smooth surface, the sea.

**āerius,** *adj.,* airy, high in the air.

**aes, aeris,** 3 *n.,* copper, money.

**aestimāti-o, -ōnis,** 3 *f.,* value.

**aestimo,** 1, value.

**aestuōsus,** *adj.,* hot, sultry.

**aet-ās, -ātis,** 3 *f.,* age, period.

**aeternus,** *adj.,* enduring, endless.

**aevum,** 2 *n.,* age, generation.

**affero, afferre, attuli, allā-tum,** 3, bring, bring tidings, announce.

**Āfricus,** *adj.,* African.

**Aganipp-ē, -ēs,** 3 *f.,* a nymph of stream on Mt. Helicon, hence the stream.

**ag-er, -ri,** 2 *m.,* land, district.

**agg-er, -eris,** 3 *m.,* mound.

**agito,** 1, drive, goad, be engaged or set in violent motion.

**ago, agere, ēgi, actum,** 3, lead, urge, perform.

**agricola,** 1 *m.,* farmer.

**aio,** 3 *defect.,* affirm, assert.

**albus,** *adj.,* white.

**āl-es, -itis,** 3 *c.,* bird, omen.

**alga,** 1 *f.,* seaweed.

**ali-quis, -qua, -quid,** *pron.,* someone, something.

**ali-us, -a, -ud,** *adj.,* other.

**allocūti-o, -ōnis,** 3 *f.,* talk, consolation.

**alloqu-or, -i, allocūtus sum,** 3 *dep.,* address.

**allū-do, -dere, -si, -sum,** 3, play, sport.

**allu-o, -ere, -i, —,** 3, wash against.

**alnus,** 2 *f.,* alder.

**al-o, -ere, -ui, -tum,** 3, feed, nourish, support.

**Alp-es, -ium,** 3 *m. pl.,* the Alps.

**alter, -a, -um,** *adj.,* the one, the other (of two).

**altus,** *adj.,* high, deep.

**amābil-is, -e,** *adj.,* lovable, charming.

**Amādry-as, -adis,** 3 *f.,* hamadryad, wood nymph.

**amāracus,** 2 *m.,* marjoram.

**amāritiēs,** 5 *f.,* bitterness, harshness.

**Amastr-is, -is,** 3 *f.,* a port on the Black Sea.

**amb-o, -ae, -o,** *adj.,* both.

**amīca,** 1 *f.,* girl friend.

**amīcitia,** 1 *f.,* friendship.

**amictus,** 4 *m.,* outer garment, cloak.

**amīcus,** 2 *m.,* friend.

**ā-mitto, -mittere, -mīsi, -missum,** 3, lose.

**amn-is, -is,** 3 *m.,* river, stream.

**amo,** 1, love.

**am-or, -ōris,** 3 *m.,* love ; *pl.,* one's loved one.

**amplificē,** *adv.,* splendidly.

**amplius,** *adv.,* more, further.

**an,** *conj.,* or.

**anc-eps, -ipitis,** *adj.,* two-headed, two-edged.

**anhēlo,** 1, breathe hard, pant.

**anīlit-ās, -ātis,** 3 *f.,* old age (of a woman).

**anima,** 1 *f.,* breeze, life, soul.

**animus,** 2 *m.,* mind, feeling.

**annu-o, -ere, -i, —,** 3, nod, assent.

**annus,** 2 *m.,* year.

**annuus,** *adj.,* lasting a year, yearly.

**ante,** *adv.* before; *prep. with acc.,* before.

**anteā,** *adv.,* formerly.

**antīquē,** *adv.,* as of old, in ancient times.

**antist-o, -āre, -eti, —,** 1, excel, surpass.

**Antius,** 2 *m.,* Antius, a plaintiff or a candidate.

**anus,** 4 *f.,* old woman (*sometimes used as adj.*).

**anxius,** *adj.,* troubled, troublesome.

**Āonius,** *adj.,* of Aonia, a part of Bœotia around Mt. Helicon, where the Muses dwelt ; of the Muses.

**aper-io, -īre, -ui, -tum,** 4, disclose, open.

**Aphēliōt-ēs, -ae,** 1 *m.,* the east wind.

**applic-o, -āre, -āvi** *or* **-ui, -ātum** *or* **-itum,** 1, join, place up against.

**approbāti-o, -ōnis,** 3 *f.,* approval.

**approbo,** 1, approve, win approval.

**apud,** *prep. with acc.,* at the house of, among.

**aqua,** 1 *f.,* water.

**Aquīnus,** 2, Aquinus (a bad poet).

**āra,** 1 *f.,* altar.

**Arab-s, -is,** *adj.,* Arabian.

**arānea,** 1 *f.,* spider, cobweb.

**arātrum,** 2 *n.,* plough.

**arbitror,** 1 *dep.,* decide, think.

**arb-or, -oris,** 3 *f.,* tree.

**Arcad-es, -um,** 3 *m. pl.,* Arcadians, shepherds.

**ar-deo, -dēre, -si, —,** 2, burn (*intrans.*), be on fire.

**ard-or, -ōris,** 3 *m.,* fire, heat.

**Ariadna,** 1, Ariadne, the daughter of Minos.

**āridus,** *adj.,* dry.

**arista,** 1 *f.,* ear of corn.

**armātus,** *adj.,* armed.

**Arrius,** 2 *m.,* an affected young man at Rome.

**ars, artis,** 3 *f.,* skill, art.

**artūs,** 4 *m. pl.,* joints, limbs.

**arvum,** 2 *n.,* field, region.

**as, assis,** 3 *m.,* a copper coin.

**Asia,** 1 *f.,* a Roman province, covering part of modern Turkey.

**Asinius,** 2 *m.,* friend of Catullus, and brother of Pollio.

**asinus,** 2 *m.,* ass.

**asp-icio, -icere, -exi, -ectum,** 3, look at, observe.

**asservo,** 1, keep, preserve.

**assiduē,** *adv.,* continually.

**assiduus,** *adj.,* continual.

**at,** *conj.,* but. Also used to introduce a curse.

**āt-er, -ra, -rum,** *adj.,* black.

**atque,** *conj.,* and.

**att-ingo, -ingere, -igi, -actum,** 3, touch, lay hand on, affect, deal with, concern.

**attrib-uo, -uere, -ui, -ūtum,** 3, assign.

**aud-ax, -ācis,** *adj.,* bold, overbold.

**aud-eo, -ēre, ausus sum,** 2 *semi-dep.,* dare.

**audio,** 4, hear, listen to.

**aufero, auferre, abstuli, ablātum,** 3, to take away, steal.

**aura,** 1 *f.,* breeze, wind.

**Aurēlius,** 2 *m.,* Aurelius, one of Catullus's circle.

**aureolus,** *adj.,* golden.

**aureus,** *adj.,* golden.

**aur-is, -is,** 3 *f.,* ear.

**aurōra,** 1 *f.,* daybreak, the east.

**Aurunculeia,** 1 *f.,* Aurunculeia, the cognomen of Vinia, bride of Manlius.

**auspicātus,** *adj.,* fortunate, well-omened.

**auspicium,** 2 *n.,* auspices, omen.

**Aust-er, -ri,** 2 *m.,* the south wind.

**aut,** *conj.,* or.

**autumo,** 1, assert.

**avē** (*imperative*), hail !

**ā-vello, -vellere, -velli** *or* **-vulsi, -vulsum,** 3, tear away.

**aveo,** 2, be eager.

**āver-to, -tere, -ti, -sum, 3,** turn away.

**avia, 1 *f.*,** grandmother.

**avunculus, 2 *m.*,** maternal uncle.

**avus, 2 *m.*,** grandfather.

**axula, 1 *f.*,** plank.

## B

**bacchan-s, -tis, 3 *f.*,** bacchante, priestess of Bacchus.

**bāsiāti-o, -ōnis, 3 *f.*,** kiss.

**bāsio, 1,** kiss.

**bāsium, 2 *n.*,** kiss.

**Battiad-ēs, -ae, 1 *m.*,** an inhabitant of Cyrene, hence the poet Callimachus.

**Battus, 2 *m.*,** Battus, the founder of Cyrene.

**beātē, *adv.*,** happily, fortunately.

**beātus, *adj.*,** happy, fortunate.

**bellē, *adv.*,** prettily.

**bellum, 2 *n.*,** war.

**bellus, *adj.*,** pretty, charming.

**bene, *adv.*,** well.

**benefactum, 2 *n.*,** a favour, a kindness.

**benignē, *adv.*,** kindly.

**bīmulus, *adj.*,** only two years old.

**Bīthȳnia, 1 *f.*,** a province in the north of Asia Minor.

**Bīthȳnus, 2 *m.*,** a Bithynian.

**bonus, *adj.*,** good.

**Bore-ās, -ae, 1 *m.*,** the north wind.

**bracchiolum, 2 *n.*,** a small arm ; *dim.* of **bracchium.**

**bracchium, 2 *n.*,** arm.

**brev-is, -e, *adj.*,** short, brief.

**Britannia, 1 *f.*,** Britain.

**Britannus, *adj.*,** British.

**bustum, 2 *n.*,** a funeral pyre.

**buxifer, -a, -um, *adj.*,** bearing box trees.

## C

**cachinnus, 2 *m.*,** loud laughter, joke.

**cacūm-en, -inis, 3 *n.*,** peak, summit.

**cado, cadere, cecidi, cāsum, 3,** fall, sink, happen.

**caed-ēs, -is, 3 *f.*,** slaughter.

**caedo, caedere, cecīdi, caesum, 3,** cut down, kill.

**caelicola, 1 *m.*,** dweller in heaven, a god.

**caelit-ēs, -um, 3 *m. pl.*,** dwellers in heaven, the gods.

**caelum, 2 *n.*,** heaven, sky.

**caenum, 2 *n.*,** dirt, filth, mud.

**Caesar, -is, 3 *m.*,** Julius Caesar.

**Caesius, 2 *m.*,** Caesius, a bad poet.

**caesius, *adj.*,** grey-eyed, cat-eyed.

**calamus, 2 *m.*,** reed, cane.

**Calvus, 2 *m.*,** Calvus, a close friend of Catullus.

**campus, 2 *m.*,** field.

**candidus, *adj.*,** white, bright, frank.

**cano, canere, cecini, cantum, 3,** sing.

**canto, 1,** sing.

**cānus, *adj.*,** white, hoary, grey.

**cap-io, -ere, cēpi, captum, 3,** take, seize.

**caprimulgus, 2 *m.*,** goat-herd, country bumpkin.

**capto, 1,** snatch at, strive after.

**cap-ut, -itis, 3 *n.*,** head.

**carm-en, -inis, 3 *n.*,** song, poem.

**carp-o, -ere, -si, -tum, 3,** pick, pluck.

**carta, *see* charta.**

**cārus, *adj.*,** dear, precious.

**Cast-or, -oris, 3 *m.*,** Castor, one

of the twin sons of Leda, and brother of Pollux.

**castus**, *adj.*, clean, pure, chaste.

**caterva**, 1 *f.*, crowd, troop.

**Catullus**, 2 *m.*, the poet.

**caveo, cavēre, cāvi, cautum**, 2, take care, beware.

**cavus**, *adj.*, hollow, hollowed.

**cē-do, -dere, -ssi, -ssum**, 3, go, yield, depart.

**celebro**, 1, frequent, haunt, celebrate in song.

**celer, -is, -e,** *adj.*, swift.

**celero**, 1, hast'n.

**cēna**, 1 *f.*, dinner.

**cēno**, 1, dine.

**centum**, *indecl. adj.*, hundred.

**Cer-ēs, -eris**, 3 *f.*, Ceres, goddess of agriculture.

**cerno, cernere, crēvi, crētum**, 3, distinguish, perceive.

**certām-en, -inis**, 3 *n.*, struggle, contest.

**certātim**, *adv.*, in rivalry.

**certē**, *adv.*, certainly, surely.

**cerva**, 1 *f.*, deer.

**charta**, 1 *f.*, paper, poem, book.

**Chīr-on, -ōnis**, 3 *m.*, Chiron, a centaur.

**chorēa**, 1 *f.*, dance.

**chorus**, 2 *m.*, dance, band of singers or dancers, chorus.

**cibus**, 2 *m.*, food.

**cinaedus**, 2 *m.*, a wanton person; also *adj.*

**cin-go, -gere, -xi, -ctum**, 3, surround, gird.

**cin-is, -eris**, 3 *m.*, ashes.

**Cinna**, 1 *m.*, Cinna, a Roman poet.

**circumd-o, -are, -edi, -atum**, 1, surround.

**circumsil-io, -īre, —, —**, 4, dance around.

**cito**, 1, call, summon.

**citus**, *adj.*, quick, rapid.

**clārus**, *adj.*, clear, famous.

**class-is, -is**, 3 *f.*, fleet.

**clau-do, -dere, -si, -sum**, 3, shut.

**claustrum**, 2 *n.*, barrier, fastening of a door.

**clēmen-s, -tis,** *adj.*, gentle, calm.

**clien-s, -tis**, 3 *m.*, dependant, client.

**coacervo**, 1, to heap up.

**coep-i, -isse, -tum**, 3 *defect.*, begin.

**coetus**, 4 *m.*, company.

**cōgitāti-o, -ōnis**, 3 *f.*, thinking, thought, plan.

**cōgito**, 1, consider, intend.

**cognitus**, *adj.*, known, well-known.

**cogn-osco, -oscere, -ōvi, -itum**, 3, learn, (*perf. tenses*) know.

**cōgo, cōgere, coēgi, coactum**, 3, collect, compel.

**cohor-s, -tis**, 3 *f.*, company, retinue, staff.

**col-ligo, -ligere, -lēgi, -lectum**, 3, collect.

**coll-is, -is**, 3 *m.*, hill, mountain.

**colloco**, 1, place, arrange.

**collum**, 2 *n.*, neck.

**col-o, -ere, -ui, cultum**, 3, cultivate, worship, inhabit.

**colōro**, 1, colour.

**Colōnia**, 1 *f.*, Colonia, town near Verona.

**colōnia**, 1 *f.*, colony.

**coma**, 1 *f.*, hair, leaf.

**comātus**, *adj.*, long-haired, in leaf.

**com-es, -itis**, 3 *c.*, comrade.

**commodo**, 1, lend.

**commodum**, 2 *n.*, favourable circumstances, advantage, reward.

**commodus,** *adj.*, suitable, convenient.

**comparo,** 1, get together, compare.

**comple-ctor, -cti, -xus sum,** 3 *dep.*, embrace.

**complexus,** 4 *m.*, embrace.

**concin-o, -ere, -ui, —,** 3, sing in concert, sing.

**concordia,** 1 *f.*, harmony, union.

**con-fero, -ferre, -tuli, collā-tum,** 3, bring together, compare.

**confestim,** *adv.*, at once, without delay.

**con-ficio, -ficere, -fēci, -fectum,** 3, construct, complete, wear out.

**confit-eor, -ēri, confessus sum,** 2 *dep.*, acknowledge, confess.

**con-jungo, -jungere, -junxi, -junctum,** 3, unite, compose.

**conj-unx, -ugis,** 3 *c.*, husband, wife.

**conscius,** *adj.*, knowing, sharing a secret.

**consp-icio, -icere, -exi, -ectum,** 3, see, gaze at.

**con-surgo, -surgere, -surrexi, -surrectum,** 3, arise.

**conte-go, -gere, -xi, -ctum,** 3, cover, conceal.

**conten-do, -dere, -di, -tum,** 3, strive, hurry.

**cont-ingo, -ingere, -igi, -actum,** 3, touch, affect, happen, reach, succeed.

**continuus,** *adj.*, without interruption, continuous.

**contrā,** *adv.*, opposite, in return.

**conturbo,** 1, disorder, wipe out.

**cōnūbium,** 2 *n.*, marriage.

**con-vello, -vellere, -velli** *or* **-vulsi, -vulsum,** 3, tear up.

**con-venio, -venīre, -vēni, ventum,** 4, assemble, agree, meet, be fitting.

**convīva,** 1 *c.*, guest.

**cōpia,** 1 *f.*, supply, plenty.

**cor, -dis,** 3 *n.*, heart ; **cordi esse,** to please (*with dat.*).

**Cornēlius,** 2 *m.*, Cornelius Nepos, historian and friend of Catullus.

**Cornificius,** 2 *m.*, Cornificius, friend of Catullus.

**corolla,** 1 *f.*, a little garland : *dim.* of **corōna.**

**corōna,** 1 *f.*, crown, garland, circle of bystanders.

**corp-us, -oris,** 3 *n.*, body.

**crēd-o, -ere, -idi, -itum,** 3, entrust (*dat. of pers.*), believe.

**creo,** 1, create, produce, make, appoint.

**cresc-o, -ere, crēvi, crētum,** 3, grow, increase.

**crīm-en, -inis,** 3 *n.*, charge, accusation, crime.

**crīn-is, -is,** 3 *m.*, hair.

**crūdēl-is, -e,** *adj.*, cruel.

**crūs, crūris,** 3 *n.*, leg.

**cubīl-e, -is,** 3 *n.*, couch, bed.

**culpa,** 1 *f.*, fault, blame.

**cult-or, -ōris,** 3 *m.*, cultivator, worshipper.

**cum,** *prep. with abl.*, with ; *conj.*, when, since, though.

**cupidē,** *adv.*, eagerly, passionately.

**cupīd-o, -inis,** 3 *f.*, love, desire.

**Cupīd-o, -inis,** 3 *m.*, Cupid, the god of love.

**cupidus,** *adj.*, loving, eager.

**cup-io, -ere, -īvi, -ītum,** 3, desire.

cupressus, 2 *f.*, cypress tree.
cūr, *adv.*, why?
cūra, 1 *f.*, care.
cūriōsus, *adj.*, careful, inquisitive.
cūro, 1, take care of.
curr-o, -ere, cucurri, cursum, 3, run.
cursus, 4 *m.*, course.
curvus, *adj.*, crooked, bent, curved.
Cybel-ē, -ēs, 3 *f.*, Cybele, a Phrygian goddess worshipped at Rome.
Cȳclad-es, -um, 3 *f. pl.*, a group of islands in the Aegean.
cymbalum, 2 *n.*, cymbal.
Cȳrēnē, -ēs, 3 *f.*, Cyrene, a Greek colony in N. Africa.
Cytōrius, *adj.*, of Cytorus.
Cytōrus, 2 *m.*, a mountain in Paphlagonia.

## D

Dardania, 1 *f.*, Troy.
Dauli-as, -adis, 3 *f.*, the Daulian bird, i.e. Procne.
dē, *prep. with abl.*, down from, concerning.
dea, 1 *f.*, goddess.
dēcē-do, -dere, -ssi, -ssum, 3, retire, give place, yield.
decem, *num. adj.*, ten.
dec-et, -ēre, -uit, 2 *impers.*, is fitting, is suitable.
decoro, 1, beautify, adorn.
dēcursus, 4 *m.*, downward course, raid.
dec-us, -oris, 3 *n.*, grace, adornment, honour.
dēdico, 1, consecrate.
dēd-o, -ere, -idi, -itum, 3, give up, surrender.
dēdū-co, -cere, -xi, -ctum, 3,

bring down, lead out, reduce, escort.
dē-ferro, -ferre, -tuli, -lātum, 3, carry down, carry away, confer upon.
dēfessus, *adj.*, exhausted.
dēfle-cto, -ctere, -xi, -xum, 3, bend.
dēflōr-esco, -escere, -ui, —, 3, fade.
dein, deinde, *adv.*, then, next.
dēlāb-or, -i, dēlapsus sum, 3 *dep.*, sink, slip down.
dēlicātus, *adj.*, fond of pleasure.
dēliciae, 1 *f. pl.*, a delight, sweetheart.
Dēlius, *adj.*, of Delos.
Delphi, 2 *m. pl.*, men of Delphi.
dēmāno, 1, flow down.
dēme-to, -tere, -ssui, -ssum, 3, mow, reap.
dēnique, *adv.*, finally, at last
den-s, -tis, 3 *m.*, tooth.
densus, *adj.*, close, thick.
dentātus, *adj.*, having fine teeth.
dēper-eo, -īre, -ii, —, 4, go to destruction, be ruined, die of love for.
dē-pōno, -pōnere, -posui, -positum, 3, put down, lay aside.
dēprecor, 1 *dep.*, avert by prayer, entreat for, cry mercy.
dēre-linquo, -linquere, -līqui, -lictum, 3, leave behind, forsake.
dē-rigo, -rigere, -rexi, -rectum, 3, direct, rule (of lines).
dēsertus, *adj.*, deserted, waste.
dēsīderium, 2 *n.*, longing.
dēsīdero, 1, to miss, feel the want of, long for.

dēs-ino, -inere, -ii, -itum, 3, cease.

dē-sisto, -sistere, -stiti, -stitum, 3, leave off.

despon-deo, -dēre, -di, -sum, 2, promise.

despu-o, -ere, —, —, 3, spit out, reject.

destinātus, *adj.*, fixed, determined.

deus, 2 *m.*, god.

dēvoro, 1, consume.

dext-er, -ra *or* -era, -rum *or* -erum, right.

dextra, 1 *f.*, right hand.

Dīa, 1 *f.*, ancient name of Naxos, a Greek island in the Aegean.

Diāna, 1 *f.*, Diana, goddess of the moon.

dic-ax, -ācis, *adj.*, witty.

dī-co, -cere, -xi, -ctum, 3, say, speak.

dictum, 2 *n.*, word.

diēs, 5 *m.*, (*sometimes f.*) day.

difficil-is, -e, *adj.*, difficult.

dif-fundo, -fundere, -fūdi, -fūsum, 3, pour out.

digitus, 2 *m.*, finger.

dignor, 1 *dep.*, think worthy of (*with abl.*).

dīligenter, *adv.*, carefully.

dī-ligo, -ligere, -lexi, -lectum, 3, value, love.

Dindymus, 2 *m.*, a mountain in Phrygia.

discē-do, -dere, -ssi, -ssum, 3, go apart, depart.

discor-s, -dis, *adj.*, at variance, contradictory.

disertus, *adj.*, eloquent, clever, shrewd.

disper-eo, -īre, -ii, —, 4, perish.

diū, *adv.*, for a long time.

dīversus, *adj.*, turned different ways.

dī-ves, -itis, *adj.*, rich.

dīvīnus, *adj.*, divine, godlike.

dīvus, 2 *m.*, a god ; *adj.*, divine.

do, dare, dedi, datum, 1, give.

doctus, *adj.*, skilled, cultured.

dol-eo, -ēre, -ui, —, 2, be in pain, grieve.

dol-or, -ōris, 3 *m.*, pain, distress.

domina, 1 *f.*, mistress.

dominus, 2 *m.*, lord, master.

domus, 2 *and* 4 *f.*, house, home.

dōno, 1, give, bestow.

dōnum, 2 *n.*, gift.

Dōrius, *adj.*, Dorian.

dormio, 4, sleep.

ducentī, *adj.*, two hundred.

dū-co, -cere, -xi, -ctum, 3, lead, think, consider.

dulc-is, -e, *adj.*, sweet, charming.

dum, *conj.*, while.

dux, ducis, *c.*, leader, chief.

### E

ē, ex, *prep. with abl.*, from, out of.

ēbrius, *adj.*, drunken, intoxicated with love.

edo, esse, ēdi, ēsum, 3, eat.

ēd-o, -ere, -idi, -itum, 3, produce, declare.

ē-duco, 1, nourish.

ef-fero, -ferre, extuli, ēlātum, 3, bring forth, make known, extol.

ef-ficio, -ficere, -fēci, -fectum, 3, accomplish.

effigiēs, 5 *f.*, likeness, image.

efflu-o, -ere, -xi, —, 3, flow out, pass away.

**ef-fundo, -fundere, -fūdi, -fū-sum,** 3, to pour forth, produce abundantly.

**ēgelidus,** *adj.*, no longer cold.

**Egnātius,** 2 *m.*, Egnatius, a Spaniard disliked by Catullus.

**ego, mei,** *pron.*, I.

**ēgregius,** *adj.*, distinguished.

**ēheu,** *interj.*, alas!

**ēlega-ns, -ntis,** *adj.*, fastidious, choice.

**Ēmathia,** 1 *f.*, Thessaly.

**ēn,** *interj.*, lo! behold!

**enim,** *conj.*, for.

**ēnit-eo, -ēre, -ui, —,** 2, shine forth.

**ēnīt-or, -i, ēnixus** *or* **ēnīsus sum,** 3 *dep.*, struggle, climb, strive.

**eo, īre, ii** *or* **īvi, itum,** 4, go.

**Eōus,** *adj.*, of dawn, eastern.

**epithalamium,** 2 *n.*, wedding hymn.

**ē-ripio, -ripere, -ripui, -rep-tum,** 3, snatch away.

**erro,** 1, wander, stray, be mistaken.

**err-or, -ōris,** 3 *m.*, mistake.

**et,** *conj.*, and, also, even.

**etiam,** *adv.*, also, even.

**Etruscus,** *adj.*, Etruscan.

**etsi,** *conj.*, although.

**excelsus,** *adj.*, lofty, distinguished.

**excio,** 4, arouse, disturb.

**ex-cipio, -cipere, -cēpi, -cep-tum,** 3, take up, receive.

**excito,** 1, arouse, stimulate.

**excrucio,** 1, torment, torture.

**ex-cutio, -cutere, -cussi, -cus-sum,** 3, shake off.

**exerceo,** 2, train, exercise, employ.

**eximius,** *adj.*, outstanding, excellent.

**exor-ior, -īri, exortus sum,** 4 *dep.*, arise.

**ex-pello, -pellere, -puli, -pul-sum,** 3, drive out.

**exper-s, -tis,** *adj.*, having no part in, devoid of.

**expl-eo, -ēre, -ēvi, -ētum,** 2, fill up, complete, satisfy.

**explic-o, -āre, -āvi** *or* **-ui, -ātum** *or* **-itum,** 1, unfold.

**expolio,** 4, polish.

**ex-primo, -primere, -pressi, -pressum,** 3, press out, express, translate.

**exprōm-o, -ere, -psi, -ptum,** 3, fetch out, display, declare.

**exspecto,** 1, await.

**exsp-uo, -uere, -ui, -ūtum,** 3, spit out.

**exstin-guo, -guere, -xi, -ctum,** 3, quench, extinguish, destroy.

**exsulto,** 1, leap up, exalt, boast.

**extoll-o, -ere, —, —,** 3, raise, exalt.

**extrēmus,** *adj.*, farthest, last, extreme.

## F

**Fabullus,** 2, Fabullus, a friend of Catullus.

**facētiae,** 1 *f. pl.*, witticisms, humour.

**facil-is, -e,** *adj.*, easy.

**facio, facere, fēci, factum,** 3, make, do.

**factum,** 2 *n.*, deed.

**fāgus,** 2 *f.*, beech tree.

**fall-ax, -ācis,** *adj.*, deceitful.

**fallo, fallere, fefelli, falsum,** 3, deceive, beguile.

**fāma,** 1 f., report, reputation, fame.

**fandus,** *adj.*, fit to be uttered, lawful.

**fās**, *indec.*, *n.*, divine law ; **fās est**, it is lawful.

**fascino**, 1, enchant, bewitch.

**fat-eor**, **-ēri**, **fassus sum**, 2 *dep.*, confess, admit.

**fātum**, 2 *n.*, fate, misfortune.

**faustus**, *adj.*, favourable, well-omened.

**fav-eo**, **-ēre**, **fāvi**, **fautum**, 2, favour, be favourable (*with dat.*).

**Favōnius**, 2 *m.*, west wind.

**fax**, **facis**, 3 *f.*, torch.

**fēcundus**, *adj.*, fertile, abundant, rich.

**fēl-ix**, **-īcis**, *adj.*, fortunate, happy.

**fēmina**, 1 *f.*, woman.

**fero**, **ferre**, **tuli**, **lātum**, 3, bear, carry ; **ferunt**, they say.

**ferreus**, *adj.*, iron.

**ferus**, *adj.*, wild, untamed.

**Fescennīnus**, *adj.*, of Fescennia, an Etruscan town, famous for its rustic verses.

**fessus**, *adj.*, tired.

**festus**, *adj.*, festive, festal.

**fētus**, 4 *m.*, offspring, fruit.

**fidēl-is**, **-e**, *adj.*, faithful.

**fidēs**, 5 *f.*, faith.

**figūra**, 1 *f.*, shape, figure, form.

**fīlius**, 2 *m.*, son.

**fīlum**, 2 *n.*, thread.

**fīo**, **fieri**, **factus sum**, 3 *semi-dep.* (*pass. of* **facio**), become, be made.

**firmo**, 1, strengthen.

**flagellum**, 2 *n.*, whip.

**flām-en**, **-inis**, 3 *n.*, blast, breeze.

**flamma**, 1 *f.*, flame.

**flammātus**, *adj.*, kindled, set on fire.

**flammeum**, 2 *n.*, bridal veil.

**flammeus**, *adj.*, fiery, fire-coloured.

**flātus**, 4 *m.*, blowing, breathing.

**flāven-s**, **-tis**, *adj.*, golden, yellow.

**flāvus**, *adj.*, golden, yellow.

**fl-eo**, **-ēre**, **-ēvi**, **-ētum**, 2, weep.

**flētus**, 4 *m.*, weeping.

**flexanimus**, *adj.*, moving, affecting (the heart).

**flōridulus**, *adj.*, blooming.

**flōridus**, *adj.*, full of flowers, blooming.

**flōs**, **flōris**, 3 *m.*, flower.

**fluctuo**, 1, undulate, move in waves, be restless.

**fluctus**, 4 *m.*, wave.

**fluentisonus**, *adj.*, resounding with waves.

**fluito**, 1, flow, float.

**flūm-en**, **-inis**, 3 *n.*, river.

**flu-o**, **-ere**, **-xi**, **-xum**, 3, flow, pass away.

**foed-us**, **-eris**, 3 *n.*, bond, compact.

**for-is**, **-is**, 3 *f.*, door.

**formōsus**, *adj.*, beautiful.

**for-s**, **-tis**, 3 *f.*, chance, fortune.

**fortasse**, *adv.*, perhaps.

**fort-is**, **-e**, *adj.*, strong, bold.

**fortūna**, 1 *f.*, chance, fortune.

**forum**, 2 *n.*, market place, public square.

**fossa**, 1 *f.*, ditch.

**foss-or**, **-ōris**, 3 *m.*, digger, ditcher, rustic.

**frang-o**, **-ere**, **frēgi**, **fractum**, 3, break, crush.

**frāt-er**, **-ris**, 3 *m.*, brother.

**frāternus**, *adj.*, brotherly.

**frequen-s**, **-tis**, *adj.*, in great numbers, assiduous.

**fretum**, 2 *n.*, channel, sea.

**frīgero**, 1, cool, refresh.

**frīgidus,** *adj.*, cool, chilly.
**frīg-us, -oris,** 3 *n.*, cold.
**(frux), frūgis,** 3 *f.*, fruit.
**fug-io, -ere, fūgi, fugitum,** 3, flee, go into exile.
**fugo,** 1, put to flight.
**ful-geo, -gēre, -si, —,** 2, flash, glitter.
**fūmo,** 1, smoke.
**fundus,** 2 *m.*, farm.
**fūn-us, -eris,** 3 *n.*, funeral rites.
**furibundus,** *adj.*, raging.
**Fūrius,** 2 *m.*, Furius, a member of Catullus's circle.
**fur-or, -ōris,** 3 *m.*, rage, fury.
**furtīvus,** *adj.*, stolen, secret.
**furtum,** 2 *n.*, theft, crafty deceit.
**fūsus,** 2 *m.*, spindle.

## G

**Gāius,** 2 *m.*, Gaius.
**Galla,** 1 *f.*, a priest of Cybele.
**Gallicus,** *adj.*, of Gaul, Gallic.
**gaud-eo, -ēre, gāvīsus sum,** 2 *semi-dep.*, rejoice.
**gaudium,** 2 *n.*, joy.
**gemellus,** *adj.*, twin.
**geminus,** *adj.*, twin.
**gem-o, -ere, -ui, -itum,** 3, sigh, groan.
**gen-er, -eri,** 2 *m.*, son-in-law.
**genit-or, -ōris,** 3 *m.*, father, creator.
**gen-s, -tis,** 3 *f.*, race, nation.
**gen-us, -eris,** 3 *n.*, family, race, kind.
**ger-o, -ere, gessi, gestum,** 3, bear, carry on, perform.
**gestio,** 4, exult.
**grabātus,** 2 *m.*, pallet, camp-bed.
**grad-ior, -i, gressus sum,** 3 *dep.*, walk, go.
**grātēs,** 3 *f. pl.*, thanks.

**grātia,** 1 *f.*, favour, friendship, thanks.
**grātus,** *adj.*, dear, pleasing, thankful.
**gravēd-o, -inis,** 3 *f.*, heaviness in the head, a cold.
**grav-is, -e,** *adj.*, heavy, grievous.
**graviter,** *adv.*, heavily, grievously, seriously.
**gremium,** 2 *n.*, lap, bosom.
**gurg-es, -itis,** 3 *m.*, abyss, gulf, torrent.

## H

**habeo,** 2, have, hold.
**haedus,** 2 *m.*, young goat, kid.
**Hamādry-as, -adis,** 3 *f.*, wood-nymph.
**harēna,** 1 *f.*, sand, arena.
**haud,** *adv.*, not.
**hedera,** 1 *f.*, ivy.
**hederiger, -a, -um,** *adj.*, ivy-bearing.
**Helicōnius,** *adj.*, of Mount Helicon.
**Hellespontus,** 2 *m.*, the Hellespont (Dardanelles).
**hendecasyllabi,** 2 *m. pl.*, verses of eleven syllables.
**hera,** 1 *f.*, mistress.
**hercule,** *interj.*, by Hercules !
**hēr-ēs, -ēdis,** *c.*, heir, heiress.
**bēr-ōs, -ōis,** 3 *m.*, hero.
**herus,** 2 *m.*, master.
**Hesperus,** 2 *m.*, the evening star.
**hesternus,** *adj.*, of yesterday.
**heu,** *interj.*, alas!
**Hibērus,** *adj.*, Iberian, Spanish.
**hīc, haec, hōc,** *pron. and adj.*, this ; he, she, it.
**hīc,** *adv.*, here, at this point.
**hilar-is, -e,** *adj.*, gay, cheerful
**hinc,** *adv.*, hence.

**hom-o, -inis,** 3 *m.,* man.
**hōra,** 1 *f.,* hour.
**horribil-is, -e,** *adj.,* terrible, dreadful.
**horridus,** *adj.,* savage, uncouth.
**horrifico,** 1, ruffle, roughen.
**horrificus,** *adj.,* terrifying, appalling.
**Hortalus,** 2 *m.,* Hortalus (*v.* poem 11).
**hortor,** 1 *dep.,* incite, instigate, exhort.
**hortulus,** 2 *m., dim.* of **hortus,** garden.
**hortus,** 2 *m.,* garden.
**hosp-es, -itis,** 3 *m.,* host, guest, stranger.
**host-is, -is,** 3 *m.,* enemy.
**hūc,** *adv.,* to this place.
**humus,** 2 *f.,* earth, ground.
**hyacinthinus,** *adj.,* belonging to the hyacinth.
**hyacinthus,** 2 *m.,* hyacinth (our blue iris).
**Hӯm-en, -enis,** 3, *and* **Hymenaeus,** 2, the god of marriage.
**Hyrcāni,** 2 *m. pl.,* a people who lived by the Caspian Sea.

### I

**ibi,** *adv.,* there.
**Īda,** 1 *f.,* mountain range of Asia Minor.
**Īdalium,** 2 *n.,* a city in Cyprus sacred to Venus.
**īdem, eadem, idem,** *pron. and adj.,* the same.
**identidem,** *adv.,* repeatedly, continually.
**ign-is, -is,** 3 *m.,* fire.
**ign-osco, -oscere, -ōvi, -ōtum,** 3, pardon (*with dat.*).
**ignōtus,** *adj.,* unknown.

**ille, illa, illud,** *pron. and adj.,* that.
**illepidus,** *adj.,* rude, ill-mannered.
**illīc,** *adv.,* there.
**illinc,** *adv.,* thence.
**illūc,** *adv.,* to that place, thither.
**imb-er, -ris,** 3 *m.,* shower.
**imb-uo, -uere, -ui, -ūtum,** 3, saturate, dye.
**immātūrus,** *adj.,* untimely, premature.
**immemor, -is,** *adj.,* unmindful, forgetful.
**immeren-s, -tis,** *adj.,* undeserving, innocent.
**immineo,** 2, overhang, be near to, menace.
**immo,** *adv.,* no indeed ; **immo vero,** *adv.,* nay rather.
**impend-eo, -ēre, —, —,** 2, overhang, impend, threaten.
**impensē,** *adv.,* exceedingly, eagerly.
**impetus,** 4 *m.,* attack, speed, force.
**impius,** *adj.,* irreverent, wicked.
**implic-o, -āre, -āvi** *or* **-ui, -ātum** *or* **-itum,** 1, entwine, entangle, involve.
**impoten-s, -tis,** *adj.,* powerless, headstrong.
**impotentia,** 1 *f.,* helplessness, unbridled passion.
**īmus,** *adj.,* lowest, deepest, last.
**in,** *prep. with acc.,* into, in ; *with abl.,* in, on.
**incen-do, -dere, -di, -sum,** 3, kindle, arouse.
**inc-ido, -idere, -idi, -āsum,** 3, fall upon.
**incito,** 1, urge forward, encourage, stimulate.

incoho, 1, begin.

incolum-is, -e, *adj*, safe, un-
harmed.

incommodum, 2 *n*., incon-
venience, misfortune, pest.

increb-resco, -rescere, -rui,
—, 3, become frequent, in-
crease.

incultus, *adj*., uncultivated.

incurvus, *adj*., bent, crooked.

inde, *adv*., thence, thereupon.

India, 1 *f*., India.

indi-co, -cere, -xi, -ctum, 3,
publish, announce.

indidem, *adv*., from the same
place.

indignē, *adv*., unworthily, un-
deservedly.

indistinctus, *adj*., mixed, con-
fused.

indomitus, *adj*., unsubdued.

Indus, 2 *adj*., Indian.

ineptio, 4, play the fool.

ineptus, *adj*., absurd, unsuit-
able.

infacētus, *adj*., stupid, lacking
in wit.

inferiae, 1 *f. pl*., sacrifices to
the dead.

infestus, *adj*., hostile, unsafe.

infirmus, *adj*., weak.

ingenero, 1, implant.

ingenuus, *adj*., freeborn, noble,

ingrātus, *adj*., unpleasant,
thankless.

in-jicio, -jicere, -jēci, -jectum,
3, hurl, impose, inspire.

injūria, 1 *f*., insult, injury.

inquam, *defect. verb*, say.

inscius, *adj*., ignorant, un-
aware.

insidiae, 1 *f. pl*., ambush.

instar, *used as prep. with gen.*,
like.

insula, 1 *f*., island.

insulsus, *adj*., insipid, dull,
absurd.

intactus, *adj*., untouched.

integ-er, -ra, -rum, *adj*., un-
touched, whole, blameless.

inter, *prep. with acc.*, between,
among.

intereā, *adv*., meanwhile.

interi-or, -us, *adj*., inner,
middle.

interitus, 4 *m*., destruction,
death.

intimus, *adj*., innermost.

intus, *adv*., within.

invenustus, *adj*., without
charm, unattractive.

in-video, -vidēre, -vīdi, -vīs-
um, 2, envy (*with dat.*) ;
invisus, hated.

invīs-o, -ere, -i, -um, 3, visit.

invītus, *adj*., unwilling.

invoco, 1, call upon, appeal to.

Ionius, *adj*., Ionian.

ips-e, -a, -um, *pron and adj.*, self.

īrasc-or, -i, īrātus sum, 3
*dep*., be angry (*with dat.*).

irrigo, 1, water, flood, refresh.

irritus, *adj*., of no effect, void.

irrumāt-or, -ōris, 3 *m*., scoun-
drel.

is, ea, id, *pron. and adj.*, that ;
he, she, it.

ist-e, -a, -ud, *pron. and adj.*,
this, that ; he, she.

istinc, *adv*., from that place.

ita, *adv*., thus, so.

Italus, *adj*., of Italy, Italian.

item, *adv*., besides, also.

it-er, -ineris, 3 *n*., way, jour-
ney, road.

Itylus, 2 *m*., Itylus *or* Itys,
son of Tereus.

## J

jaceo, 2, lie.

jac-io, -ere, jēci, jactum, 3, throw.
jam, *adv*., now, already.
jānua, 1 *f*., door.
jocāti-o, -ōnis, 3 *f*., joke.
jocor, 1 *dep*., joke.
jocōsus, *adj*., jesting.
jocus, 2 *m*., joke.
jūcundus, *adj*., delightful, charming.
jūd-ex, -icis, 3 *m*., judge.
jugum, 2 *n*., yoke, range of mountains.
jun-go, -gere, -xi, -ctum, 3, join.
Jūn-o, -ōnis, 3 *f*., Juno, wife of Jupiter.
Juppiter, Jovis, 3 *m*., Jupiter, father of the gods.
justificus, *adj*., that acts justly.
justitia, 1 *f*., justice, righteousness.
juvenca, 1 *f*., heifer.
juvencus, 2 *m*., bullock.
juven-is, -is, 3 *m*., youth; *also adj*.
juventa, 1 *f*., youth.
juv-o, -āre, jūvi, jūtum, 1, help.

## L

labellum, 2 *n*., *dim. of* labrum, lip.
labo, 1, totter, hesitate.
lāb-or, -i, lapsus sum, 3 *dep*., glide down, perish.
lab-or, -ōris, 3 *m*., work.
labōriōsē, *adv*., laboriously, grievously.
labōriōsus, *adj*., toilsome.
lacrima, 1 *f*., tear.
lactens, *adj*., milky, milk-white.
lacus, 4 *m*., lake, pool.
lae-do, -dere, -si, -sum, 3,

laetitia, 1 *f*., joy.
laetus, *adj*., joyful, fertile, rich.
laevus, *adj*., left.
languidulus, *adj*., somewhat feeble.
langu-or, -ōris, 3 *m*., faintness, weariness.
Lānuvīnus, *adj*., of Lanuvium, a city in Central Italy.
lār, laris, 3 *m*., hearth, home; lares, *pl*., the gods of the house.
Lārius, *adj*., Larian, of the lake in N. Italy, now Como.
lāsarpīcifer, -a, -um, *adj*., silphium-bearing.
lassulus, *adj*., worn out, weary.
Lātōnia, 1 *f*., daughter of Latona, i.e. Diana.
laurus, 2 *and* 4 *f*., bay-tree.
lau-s, -dis, 3 *f*., praise.
lav-o, -āre, lāvi, lavātum, lautum *or* lōtum, 1, wash.
lectīca, 1 *f*., sedan-chair.
lectulus, 2 *m*., a small couch, bed; *dim*. of lectus.
lectus, 2 *m*., couch, bed.
leg-o, -ere, lēgi, lectum, 3, collect, select, read.
lēn-is, -e, *adj*., smooth, gentle, mild.
lēniter, *adv*., gently, moderately.
lentus, *adj*. pliant, slow.
le-o, -ōnis, 3 *m*., lion.
lepidus, *adj*., charming, elegant.
lepō-s *or* -r, -ōris, 3 *m*., grace, charm.
Lesbia, 1 *f*., Lesbia.
Lēthaeus, *adj*., of Lethe, a river of Hades.
lētifer, -a, -um, *adj*., death-bringing.
lev-is, -e, *adj*., light, trifling.

leviter, *adv.*, lightly, easily.
levo, 1, lighten, mitigate.
libellus, 2 *m.*, a little book.
libenter, *adv.*, willingly.
lib-er, -ri, 2 *m.*, book.
līber, -a, -um, *adj.*, free.
Līber, 2 *m.*, Bacchus ; Arrius's uncle.
līberi, 2 *m. pl.*, children.
lib-et, -ēre, -uit, 2 *impers.*, it pleases.
libīd-o, -inis, 3 *f.*, pleasure, desire.
librārius, 2 *m.*, bookseller.
Libya, 1 *f.*, province of N. Africa.
Libyssus, *adj.*, Libyan.
lic-et, -ēre, -uit, it is permitted (*with dat. of pers.*).
Licinius, 2 *m.*, Licinius Calvus, friend of Catullus.
ligo, 1, bind.
Ligur, -is, *adj.*, Ligurian.
līm-en, -inis, 3 *n.*, threshold, house.
limpidus, *adj.*, clear, pure.
lingua, 1 *f.*, tongue.
linqu-o, -ere, līqui, —, 3, leave.
linteum, 2 *n.*, linen, sail, handkerchief.
liquen-s, -tis, *adj.*, flowing.
lītorāl-is, -e, *adj.*, of the seashore.
litterāt-or, -ōris, 3 *m.*, grammarian, commentator.
līt-us, -oris, 3 *n.*, shore.
līvidus, *adj.*, lead-coloured, blackish.
loco, 1, place.
locus, 2 *m.*, place, *plur.* loca, *n.*
longē, *adv.*, far.
longinquus, *adj.*, distant, long-lasting.
longus, *adj.*, long, distant, tall.

loqu-or, -i, locūtus sum, 3 *dep.*, speak.
lōrum, 2 *n.*, strap.
lūc-eo, -ēre, luxi, —, 2, shine, dawn.
Lūcīna, 1 *f.*, goddess of child birth, *i.e.* Juno.
luctus, 4 *m.*, sorrow, grief.
lūdicrum, 2 *n.*, public games, game, toy.
lū-do, -dere, -si, -sum, 3, play, celebrate games.
lūdus, 2 *m.*, game, sport, school.
lū-geo, -gēre, -xi, -ctum, 2, mourn, lament.
lūm-en, -inis, 3 *n.*, light.
lūna, 1 *f.*, moon.
lūteus, *adj.*, saffron-coloured, yellow.
lutum, 2 *n.*, mud.
lux, lūcis, 3 *f.*, light.
Lȳdius, *adj.*, Lydian.

## M

made-facio, -facere, -fēci, -factum, 3, moisten, drench.
Maen-as, -adis, 3 *f.*, priestess of Bacchus, Bacchante.
maer-or, -ōris, 3 *m.*, mourning, sorrow.
maestus, *adj.*, sorrowful.
magis, *adv.*, more.
magnus, *adj.*, great.
māla, 1 *f.*, cheek.
male, *adv.*, badly, wickedly.
malignē, *adv.*, enviously.
mālo, malle, mālui, —, prefer.
mālum, 2 *n.*, apple.
malum, 2 *n.*, evil.
malus, *adj.*, bad.
man-eo, -ēre, -si, -sum, 2, stay, remain.
māno, 1, flow, trickle, spread.

mantica, 1 *f.*, bag, wallet.
manus, 4 *f.*, hand.
Marcus, 2 *m.*, Marcus, prae-
  nomen of Cicero.
mar-e, -is, 3 *n.*, sea.
marīta, 1 *f.*, wife.
marītus, 2 *m.*, husband.
Marrūcīnus, Marrucinus Asin-
  ius Pollio, brother of the
  famous A. Pollio.
māt-er, -ris, 3 *f.*, mother.
māternus, *adj.*, maternal.
mātūrus, *adj.*, ripe.
mātūtīnus, *adj.*, of the morning.
Māvor-s, -tis, 3 *m.*, Mars.
medulla, 1 *f.*, marrow.
mellītus, *adj.*, honey-sweet.
membrāna, 1 *f.*, skin, parch-
  ment.
membrum, 2 *n.*, limb.
men-s, -tis, 3 *f.*, mind, thoughts.
mensa, 1 *f.*, table.
menstruus, *adj.*, monthly.
mer-eor, -ēri, meritus sum,
  2 *dep.*, deserve.
merus, *adj.*, pure, unmixed.
mēt-ior, -īri, mensus sum,
  4 *dep.*, measure.
met-uo, -uere, -ui, -ūtum, 3,
  fear.
meus, *adj.*, my, mine.
mīca, 1 *f.*, crumb, morsel.
mic-o, -āre, -ui, —, 1, glisten,
  gleam.
mīliēs, *adv.*, a thousand times.
mille, *indec. adj.*, thousand ;
  mīlia, 3 *n. pl.*, thousands.
min-ax, -ācis, *adj.*, threatening.
Mīnō-is, -idis, 3 *f.*, daughter of
  Minos, king of Crete.
Mīnōus, *adj.*, Minoan, Cretan.
minus, *adv.*, less.
mīrificē, *adv.*, wonderfully.
mīror, 1 *dep.*, wonder, wonder
  at, admire.

mīrus, *adj.*, wonderful.
misc-eo, -ēre, -ui, mixtum, 2,
  mix.
misellus, *adj.*, wretched.
miser, -a, -um, *adj.*, wretched.
miser-eor, -ēri, -itus sum, 2
  *dep.*, pity (*with gen.*)
mīt-is, -e, soft, ripe.
mitra, 1 *f.*, headband, turban.
mitto, mittere, mīsi, missum,
  3, send, let go.
mnēmosynum, 2 *n.*, memorial,
  souvenir.
modo, *adv.*, only, just now ;
  modo . . . modo . . . some-
  times . . . sometimes . . .
modus, 2 *m.*, measure, rhythm,
  limit, manner.
moenia, 3 *n. pl.*, walls, city.
molestus, *adj.*, troublesome,
  toilsome.
moll-is, -e, *adj.*, soft, tender,
  unmanly.
moneo, 2, advise.
monimentum, 2 *n.*, memorial.
mon-s, -tis, 3 *m.*, mountain.
mora, 1 *f.*, delay, hindrance.
morbus, 2 *m.*, disease.
mord-eo, -ēre, momordi,
  morsum, 2, bite.
mor-ior, -i, mortuus sum, 3
  *dep.*, die.
moror, 1 *dep.*, delay.
mor-s, -tis, 3 *f.*, death.
morsus, 4 *m.*, bite.
mortāl-is, -e, mortal.
mōs, mōris, 3 *m.*, habit,
  custom.
mov-eo, -ēre, mōvi, mōtum,
  2, move.
mūla, 1 *f.*, mule.
mul-ceo, -cēre, -si, -sum, 2,
  stroke, soothe.
mulier, -is, 3 *f.*, woman.
multus, *adj.*, much, many.

**mūnic-eps, -ipis,** 3 *m.,* citizen (of a free town, **municipium**).

**mūn-us, -eris,** 3 *n.,* service, gift.

**Mūsa,** 1 *f.,* a Muse.

**mūto,** 1, change.

**mūtus,** *adj.,* dumb, silent.

**mūtuus,** *adj.,* reciprocal, mutual.

**myrtus,** 2 and 4 *f.,* myrtle tree.

# N

**nam, namque,** *conj.,* for.

**narro,** 1, tell, relate.

**nasc-or, -i, nātus sum,** 3 *dep.,* be born.

**nāsus,** 2 *m.,* nose.

**nāta,** 1 *f.,* daughter.

**nāti-o, -ōnis,** 3 *f.,* race, nation, tribe.

**nato,** 1, swim, float.

**nātus,** 2 *m.,* son.

**nāv-is, -is,** 3 *f.,* ship.

**nē,** *conj.,* lest.

**nec, neque,** *conj.,* neither, nor.

**necdum,** *adv.,* and not yet, nor yet.

**necesse,** *indecl. adj.,* necessary.

**nefandus,** *adj.,* unmentionable, wicked.

**nefārius,** *adj.,* abominable, wicked.

**negle-go, -gere, -xi, -ctum,** 3, disregard, neglect.

**negligen-s, -tis,** *adj.,* negligent.

**nego,** 1, deny.

**Nemes-is, -is,** 3 *f.,* goddess of retribution.

**nēm-o, nullĭus,** 3 *c.,* no-one.

**nem-us, -oris,** 3 *n.,* grove, wood.

**nep-os, -ōtis,** 3 *m.,* grandson, descendant.

**Neptūnius,** *adj.,* of Neptune.

**Neptūnus,** 2 *m.,* god of the sea.

**nequ-eo, -īre, -īvi, -itum,** 4, be unable.

**nēquīquam,** *adv.,* in vain.

**nescio,** 4, not to know, be ignorant.

**nescio-quis, -quid,** *pron.,* somebody, something.

**nescius,** *adj.,* ignorant, unaware.

**nī,** *conj.,* unless.

**Nīcaea,** 1 *f.,* Nicaea, city of Bithynia.

**nig-er, -ra, -rum,** *adj.,* black.

**nihil, nīl,** *indecl.,* nothing.

**Nīlus,** 2 *m.,* river Nile.

**nīmīrum,** *adv.,* without doubt, certainly.

**nimium,** *adv.,* too much, too.

**nisi,** *conj.,* unless.

**niteo,** 2, shine.

**nīt-or, -i, nixus** *or* **nīsus sum,** 3 *dep.,* press upon, strive, rely on (*with abl.*).

**niveus,** *adj.,* snowy, snow-white.

**no,** 1, swim, float.

**nōbil-is, -e,** *adj.,* famous.

**nōlo, nolle, nōlui, —,** be unwilling.

**nōm-en, -inis,** 3 *n.,* name.

**nōn,** *adv.,* not.

**nondum,** *adv.,* not yet.

**noscito,** 1, know, recognise.

**nosc-o, -ere, nōvi, nōtum,** 3, learn.

**nost-er, -ra, -rum,** *adj.,* our.

**nothus,** *adj.,* fake, counterfeit.

**nōtus,** *adj.,* well-known, famous.

**Novum Cōmum,** 2 *n.,* a town in Transpadane Gaul.

**novus,** *adj.,* new.

**nox, noctis,** 3 *f.,* night.

**nū-bo, -bere, -psi, -ptum,** 3, marry (*with dat.*)
**nūdus,** *adj.*, bare, naked.
**nūgae,** 1 *f. pl.*, trifles, jests.
**nullus,** *adj.*, none, no (*adj.*)
**nūm-en, -inis,** 3 *n.*, power, will, divinity.
**numero,** 1, count.
**numerus,** 2 *m.*, number.
**numquam,** *adv.*, never.
**nunc,** *adv.*, now.
**nuntio,** 1, announce.
**nuntius,** 2 *m.*, messenger.
**nūper,** *adv.*, lately.
**nupta,** 1 *f.*, bride, wife.
**nuptiāl-is, -e,** *adj.*, nuptial
**nūto,** 1, nod, waver.
**nūtrio,** 4, nourish.
**nūtr-ix, -īcis,** 3 *f.*, nurse.
**nux, nucis,** 3 *f.*, nut.
**nympha,** 1 *f.*, nymph.

## O

**obdūro,** 1, persist, endure.
**obēsus,** *adj.*, fat.
**oblīvisc-or, -i, oblītus sum,** 3 *dep.*, forget (*with gen.*).
**obs-es, -idis,** 3 *c.*, hostage.
**obstinātus,** *adj.*, stubborn.
**ob-sum, -esse, -fui,** hinder, hurt.
**obter-o, -ere, obtrīvi, obtrī-tum,** 3, bruise, crush.
**obvius,** *adj.*, in the way of, confronting (*with dat.*).
**occī-do, -dere, -di, -sum,** 3, kill.
**occ-ido, -idere, -idi, -āsum,** 3, go down, perish.
**ōceanus,** 2 *m.*, ocean, sea.
**ocellus,** 2 *m.*, *dim.* of **oculus,** eye.
**octō,** *num. adj.*, eight.
**oculus,** 2 *m.*, eye.
**ōdi, ōdisse,** 3 *defect.*, hate.

**odium,** 2 *n.*, hate.
**od-or, -ōris,** 3 *m.*, smell, scent.
**officium,** 2 *n.*, service, ceremony, duty.
**offirmo,** 1, persevere.
**olen-s, -tis,** *adj.*, sweet-smelling.
**ol-facio, -facere, -fēci, -factum,** 3, smell.
**ōlim,** *adv.*, once, formerly
**olīva,** 1 *f.*, olive-tree.
**Olympus,** 2 *m.*, Mt. Olympus, heaven, sky.
**ōm-en, -inis,** 3 *n.*, sign, omen.
**omn-is, -e,** *adj.*, all, every.
**on-us, -eris,** 3 *n.*, burden.
**opācus,** *adj.*, shady, dark.
**opera,** 1 *f.*, work, care, attention.
**oper-io, -īre, -ui, -tum,** 4, cover, close.
**oppōn-o, -ere, opposui, oppositum,** 3, place up against.
**oport-et, -ēre, -uit,** 2 *impers.*, it behoves.
**(ops), opis,** 3 *f.*, help, wealth.
**optātus,** *adj.*, desired, desirable.
**opto,** 1, desire, choose.
**op-us, -eris,** 3 *n.*, work, literary composition.
**opus,** *n.*, *indecl.*, need.
**ōra,** 1 *f.*, shore, border.
**ōrāclum,** 2 *n.*, oracle.
**ōrāti-o, -ōnis,** 3 *f.*, speech.
**ōrāt-or, -ōris,** 3 *m.*, speaker, orator.
**orbus,** *adj.*, destitute, bereaved.
**Orcus,** 2 *m.*, the lower world.
**orīg-o, -inis,** 3 *f.*, beginning, source.
**or-ior, -īri, ortus sum** 4 *dep.*, rise, begin.
**ōro,** 1, pray, entreat.
**ōs, ōris,** 3 *n.*, mouth, face.
**os, ossis,** 3 *n.*, bone.

**osten-do, -dere, -di, -tum** *or* **-sum,** 3, show.

**ostium,** 2 *n.,* door, entrance.

**ōtiōsus,** *adj.,* at leisure, unconcerned.

**ōtium,** 2 *n.,* leisure, idleness.

### P

**paene,** *adv.,* almost.

**palam,** *adv.,* openly, publicly.

**palimpsestus,** 2 *m.,* parchment.

**pallidulus,** *adj.,* rather pale.

**palma,** 1 *f.,* palm of the hand, oar-blade.

**palmula,** 1 *f., dim.* of **palma,** oar-blade.

**pal-us, -ūdis,** 3 *f.,* swamp.

**pa-ndo, -ndere, -ndi, -ssum,** 3, unfold, open.

**pang-o, -ere, panxi** *or* **pepigi, panctum** *or* **pactum,** 3, fix, settle.

**papāv-er, -eris,** 3 *n.,* poppy.

**papilla,** 1 *f.,* breast.

**papȳrus,** 2 *m.,* paper made of reed.

**pār, paris,** *adj.,* equal.

**Parca,** 1 *f.,* goddess of fate.

**parcus,** *adj.,* frugal, small.

**paren-s, -tis,** 3 *c.,* parent, ancestor.

**pār-eo,** 2, obey (*with dat.*).

**par-io, -ere, peperi, partum,** 3, bring forth, bear.

**Parnāsus,** 2 *m.,* Mt. Parnassus, sacred to Apollo.

**paro,** 1, prepare, obtain.

**par-s, -tis,** 3 *f.,* part.

**parthenic-ē, -ēs,** 3 *f.,* parthenium, a plant.

**Parthus,** *adj.,* Parthian.

**parvulus,** *adj.,* very small, tiny.

**parvus,** *adj.,* small.

**passer, -is,** 3 *m.,* sparrow.

**passim,** *adv.,* in every direction.

**pat-er, -ris,** 3 *m.,* father.

**pati-or, -i, passus sum,** 3 *dep.,* suffer, permit.

**patrōna,** 1 *f.,* protectress.

**patrōnus,** 2 *m.,* protector.

**paucus,** *adj.,* few, little.

**paulus,** *adj.,* little ; **paulum,** 2 *n.,* a little.

**peccātum,** 2 *n.,* fault, mistake.

**pect-us, -oris,** 3 *n.,* breast, heart.

**pec-us, -oris,** 3 *n.,* cattle.

**Pēl-eus, -ei,** 2 *m.,* Peleus, father of Achilles.

**Pēl-ion, -ii** *or* **-i,** 2 *n.,* a mountain in Thessaly.

**pell-o, -ere, pepuli, pulsum,** 3, beat, drive.

**Pelop-s, -is,** 3 *m.,* Pelops, grandfather of Agamemnon.

**Penāt-es, -ium,** 3 *m. pl.,* household gods.

**pend-eo, -ēre, pependi, —,** 2, hang, depend.

**Pēnelopēus,** *adj.,* of Penelope

**penetro,** 1, make way into.

**Pēnēus,** 2 *m.,* Peneus, the river god of Tempe.

**per,** *prep. with acc.,* through, by means of.

**perc-ello, -ellere, -uli,-ulsum,** 3, beat down, discourage.

**perditē,** *adv.,* recklessly, distractedly.

**perd-o, -ere, -idi, -itum,** 3, destroy, lose.

**perdū-co, -cere, -xi, -ctum,** 3, lead or bring over.

**peregrīnus,** *adj.,* foreign.

**perenn-is, -e,** *adj.,* everlasting.

**per-eo, -īre, -ii, -itum,** 4, be destroyed, perish.

**per-fero, -ferre, -tuli, -lātum,** 3, carry through, endure.

**per-fundo, -fundere, -fūdi, -fūsum,** 3, wet, drench.

**per-go, -gere, -rexi, -rectum,** 3, go forward, proceed.

**perīculum,** 2 *n.*, danger.

**perjūrus,** *adj.*, forsworn, perjured.

**permi-sceo, -scēre, -scui, -xtum,** 2, mingle, confuse.

**permul-ceo, -cēre, -si, -sum,** 2, soothe.

**perniciēs,** 5 *f.*, destruction.

**pern-ix, -īcis,** *adj.*, swift, fleet.

**pernumero,** 1, reckon, count.

**perpetuus,** *adj.*, constant, uninterrupted ; **in perpetuum,** for ever.

**persaepe,** *adv.*, very often.

**perscrī-bo, -bere, -psi, -ptum,** 3, write out in full.

**persp-icio, -icere, -exi, -ectum,** 3, look through, ascertain.

**per-vinco, -vincere, -vīci, -victum,** 3, conquer, surpass.

**pēs, pedis,** 3 *m.*, foot, metrical foot, rope attached to sail.

**pestilen-s, -tis,** *adj.*, pestilential, noxious.

**pestilentia,** 1 *f.*, pest, plague.

**pest-is, -is,** 3 *f.*, plague, destruction.

**petīt-or, -ōris,** 3 *m.*, applicant, prosecutor, candidate for office.

**pet-o, -ere, -īvi** or **-ii, -ītum,** 3, seek.

**Phaëth-on, -ontis,** 3 *m.*, Phaethon, son of Helios.

**phasēlus,** 2 *m. and f.*, yacht.

**Phrygius,** *adj.*, Phrygian, Trojan.

**piet-ās, -ātis,** 3 *f.*, duty, piety.

**pig-er, -ra, -rum,** *adj.*, lazy.

**pign-us, -oris** or **-eris,** 3 *n.*, pledge.

**pilus,** 2 *m.*, hair ; **non pili facere,** not to care a straw.

**pīneus,** *adj.*, of pine.

**pingu-is, -e,** *adj.*, fat, rich.

**pīpilo,** 1, chirp.

**pius,** *adj.*, devout, loyal, dutiful.

**plac-eo,** 2, please (*with dat.*).

**placidus,** *adj.*, gentle, calm.

**plan-go, -gere, -xi, -ctum,** 3, strike, lament, bewail.

**plang-or, -ōris,** 3 *m.*, striking, splashing.

**platanus,** 2 *f.*, plane-tree.

**plēnus,** *adj.*, full.

**plexus,** *adj.*, interwoven, plaited.

**plumbum,** 2 *n.*, lead.

**plūs,** *adv.*, more.

**poēm-a, -atis,** 3 *n.*, poem.

**poena,** 1 *f.*, punishment.

**poēta,** 1 *m.*, poet.

**Polli-o, -ōnis,** 3 *m.*, Pollio, surname of two brothers.

**poll-uo, -uere, -ui, -ūtum,** 3, defile.

**Polyxena,** 1 *f.*, Polyxena, daughter of Priam and Hecuba.

**pond-us, -eris,** 3 *n.*, weight.

**pon-s, -tis,** 3 *m.*, bridge.

**ponticulus,** 2 *m.*, *dim.* of **pons,** bridge.

**Ponticus,** *adj.*, of Pontus, the Black Sea.

**popl-es, -itis,** 3 *m.*, knee.

**por-rigo, -rigere, -rexi, -rectum,** 3, reach out, extend.

**porrō,** *adv.*, further, in future.

**porta,** 1 *f.*, gate.

**porto,** 1, carry, bring.

**possum, posse, potui,** be able.

post, *adv. and prep. with acc.*, after, behind.
posthāc, *adv.*, hereafter.
postillā, *adv.*, afterwards.
postquam, *conj.*, after, when.
postrēmō, *adv.*, at last, finally.
postrēmus, *adj.*, last, final.
poten-s, -tis, *adj.*, powerful.
potis *or* pote, *indecl. adj.*, able, possible.
prae, *prep. with abl.*, before.
praec-eps, -ipitis, *adj.*, headlong.
praecerp-o, -ere, -si, -tum, 3, gather prematurely.
praeda, 1 *f.*, booty, spoil.
praefor, 1 *dep.*, say beforehand, prophesy.
praesen-s, -tis, *adj.*, present.
praesertim, *adv.*, especially.
prae-sum, -esse, -fui, be over, have command of (*with dat.*).
praeter, *adv. and prep. with acc.*, besides.
praetereā, *adv.*, moreover.
praeter-eo, -īre, -ii, -itum, 4, pass by.
praetextātus, *adj.*, clothed in the toga praetexta or garment of boyhood.
praet-or, -ōris, 3 *m.*, governor of a Roman province.
praetrepidan-s, -tis, *adj.*, very impatient.
prātum, 2 *n.*, meadow.
preces, precum, 3 *f. pl.*, prayers.
prīmaevus, *adj.*, young, youthful.
prīmus, *adj.*, first.
princ-eps, -ipis, *adj.*, first ; *also subst.*, 3 *m.*, chief.
pri-or, -us, -ōris, *adj. comp.*, former, earlier.
priscus, *adj.*, ancient, old-fashioned.

prius, *adv.*, previously, before.
prō, *prep. with abl.*, in front of, on behalf of.
probē, *adv.*, properly, well.
proc-ax, -ācis, *adj.*, insolent, importunate.
prō-cēdo, -cēdere, -cessi, -cessum, 3, go forward, advance.
procella, 1 *f.*, storm, sudden attack.
prōcērus, *adj.*, high, tall.
procul, *adv.*, in the distance, far.
prō-cumbo, -cumbere, -cubui, —, 3, bend forward, sink to ground.
prō-curro, -currere, -cucurri *or* -curri, -cursum, 3, to run forwards.
prōd-eo, -īre, -ii, -itum, 4, come forwards, come forth.
prō-ficio, -ficere, -fēci, -fectum, 3, advance, help.
proficisc-or, -i, profectus sum, 3 *dep.*, set out.
profundus, *adj.*, deep.
prōgeniēs, 5 *f.*, race, descendants.
prō-icio, -icere, -jēci, -jectum, 3, hurl away, abandon.
prōmissum, 2 *n.*, promise.
prō-mitto, -mittere, -mīsi, -missum, 3, promise, assure.
prōnus, *adj.*, bent forward, headlong.
prope, *adv. and prep. with acc.*, near.
properip-ēs, -edis, *adj.*, swift of foot.
propero, 1, hurry.
prō-pōno, -pōnere, -posui, -positum, 3, set forth, publish.
Propont-is, -idis, 3 *f.*, Sea of Marmora.

**propter,** *adv. and prep. with acc.,* near, on account of.

**prōsil-io, -īre, -ui, —,** leap forth.

**prospecto, 1,** look forth, wait for.

**prosp-icio, -icere, -exi, -ectum, 3,** look forth, observe.

**prost-erno, -ernere, -rāvi, -rātum, 3,** cast down, overthrow.

**prōsum, prōdesse, prōfui,** benefit, profit (*with dat.*).

**prōvincia, 1 f.,** province.

**pūb-ēs, -is, 3 f.,** youth.

**pudīcitia, 1 f.,** chastity, modesty.

**pudīcus,** *adj.,* modest, chaste.

**pud-or, -ōris, 3 m.,** shame, modesty.

**puella, 1 f.,** girl.

**puellula, 1 f.,** *dim.* of **puella,** girl.

**puer, -i, 2 m.,** boy.

**puerperus,** *adj.,* belong to childbirth.

**pulch-er, -ra, -rum,** *adj.,* beautiful.

**pulvīn-ar, -āris, 3 n.,** couch.

**pulv-is, -eris, 3 m.,** dust.

**pūm-ex, -icis, 3 m.,** pumice-stone.

**pūriter,** *adv.,* purely, cleanly.

**purpureus,** *adj.,* purple, bright.

**pūrus,** *adj.,* clean, faultless.

**pūtidus,** *adj.,* rotten, stinking.

**puto, 1,** think.

## Q

**quae-ro, -rere, -sīvi, -sītum, 3,** seek, inquire.

**quaes-o, -ere, -īvi** *or* **-ii, —, 3,** beg.

**quāl-is, -e,** *adj.,* such as ; *interr.,* of what kind?

**quāl-iscumque, -ecumque,** *adj.,* of whatever kind.

**quam,** *adv.,* how, as, than.

**quamvis,** *conj.,* although, however.

**quando,** *adv. and conj.,* when? at any time.

**quandoquidem,** *conj.,* since indeed.

**quantum,** *adv.,* as greatly as, as much as.

**quantus,** *adj.,* as much as, as great as.

**quārē,** *adv.,* why?

**quasso, 1,** shake repeatedly, dash to pieces.

**quat-io, -ere, —, quassum, 3,** shake, agitate, excite.

**-que,** *encl. conj.,* and.

**qu-eo, -īre, -īvi, -itum, 4,** be able.

**qui, quae, quod,** *rel. pron.,* who, which.

**quia,** *conj.,* because

**quicumque, quaecumque, quodcumque,** *pron.,* whoever, whatever.

**quiē-s, -tis, 3 f.,** rest, sleep.

**quīdam, quaedam, quoddam,** *pron.,* a certain person.

**quīlibet, quaelibet, quodlibet** (*subst.* **quidlibet**), *pron.,* anyone you please.

**quīn,** *conj.,* but that . . . not, but that.

**quindecim,** *num. adj.,* fifteen.

**Quintia, 1 f.,** Quintia, a Roman lady.

**Quintilia, 1 f.,** Quintilia, wife of L. Calvus.

**quis, quid,** *interrog. pron.* (**quis, quae, quod,** *adj.*), who? what?

**quis, qua, quid,** *indef. pron.,* someone, anyone.

**quisquam, quicquam,** *pron.,* anyone, anything (usually after a negative).

**quisque, quaeque, quodque** (*subst.* **quidque**), *pron.,* each, every.

**quisquis, quicquid,** *pron.,* whosoever, whatsoever.

**quō,** *adv. and conj.,* whither.

**quod,** *conj.,* because.

**quōmodo,** *adv.,* in what manner, how.

**quōnam,** *adv.,* to what purpose?

**quondam,** *adv.,* once, formerly.

**quoniam,** *conj.,* since.

**quoque,** *conj.,* also.

**quot,** *indecl. adj.,* how many, as many as.

**quōvīs,** *adv.,* to any place.

## R

**rabidus,** *adj.,* raving.

**rādīcitus,** *adv.,* by the roots, utterly.

**rād-ix, -īcis,** 3 *f.,* root.

**Ramnūsius,** *see* Rhamnūsius.

**rāmulus,** 2 *m., dim.* of **rāmus,** branch.

**rāmus,** 2 *m.,* branch, twig.

**rapidus,** *adj.,* swift.

**rap-io, -ere, -ui, -tum,** 3, snatch, seize, take.

**rāsil-is, -e,** *adj.,* scraped, smooth.

**rati-o, -ōnis,** 3 *f.,* reckoning, reason, method.

**reboo,** 1, resound.

**re-cipio, -cipere, -cēpi, -ceptum,** 3, get back, receive.

**reconditus,** *adj,* hidden, secret.

**recordor,** 1 *dep.,* remember, recollect.

**recrepo,** 1, resound.

**rectus,** *adj.,* straight, erect, just.

**re-cumbo, -cumbere, cubui, —,** 3, lie down.

**recūro,** 1, restore, cure.

**redd-o, -ere, -idi, -itum,** 3, restore, reply, deliver.

**red-eo, -īre, -ii, -itum,** 4, return.

**redivīvus,** *adj.,* renewed.

**redū-co, -cere, -xi, -ctum,** 3, lead back.

**re-fero, -ferre, rettuli, relātum,** 3, bring back.

**re-ficio, -ficere, -fēci, -fectum,** 3, restore, refresh.

**refle-cto, -ctere, -xi, -xum,** 3, bend back, turn back.

**reful-geo, -gēre, -si, —,** 2, shine.

**rēgius,** *adj.,* royal.

**rel-inquo, -inquere, -īqui, -ictum,** 3, leave behind.

**re-mitto, -mittere, -mīsi, -missum,** 3, send back, relax.

**remoror,** 1 *dep.,* linger, hinder.

**remūneror,** 1 *dep.,* reward.

**rēmus,** 2, *m.,* oar.

**renīdeo,** 2, be resplendent, beam, smile.

**renovo,** 1, renew, restore.

**repente,** *adv.,* suddenly.

**reper-io, -īre, repperi, repertum,** 4, discover, find.

**re-pōno, -pōnere, -posui, -positum,** 3, replace, lay aside.

**reporto,** 1, bring back.

**reposc-o, -ere, —, —,** 3, demand.

**requi-esco, -escere, -ēvi, -ētum,** 3, rest.

**requī-ro, -rere, -sīvi, -sītum,** 3, look for, miss.

**rēs,** 5 *f.,* thing, affair, fact, advantage, wealth.

**resono,** 1, resound.

**respecto,** 1, look back, have regard for.

**respon-deo, -dēre, -di, -sum,** 2, reply, answer.

**re-tineo, -tinēre, -tinui, -tentum,** 2, keep back, maintain.

**reus,** 2 *m.,* the accused, defendant.

**revin-cio, -cīre, -xi, -ctum,** 4, bind.

**revīso, -ere, —, —,** 3, revisit.

**revoco,** 1, recall.

**rex, rēgis,** 3 *m.,* king.

**Rhamnūsius,** *adj.,* of Rhamnus, in Attica, where there was a statue of Nemesis.

**Rhēnus,** 2 *m.,* the Rhine.

**Rhodus** (usually **Rhodos**), 2 *f.,* Rhodes, an island in the S. Aegean.

**Rhoetēus,** *adj.,* of Rhoeteum in the Troad, Trojan.

**rīd-eo, -ēre, rīsi, rīsum,** 2, laugh.

**rīsus,** 4 *m.,* laughter.

**rōbustus,** *adj.,* strong, solid.

**rogo,** 1, ask.

**rogus,** 2 *m.,* funeral pile.

**Rōmulus,** 2 *m.,* Romulus, founder of Rome.

**roscidus,** *adj.,* dewy.

**rubeo,** 2, be red, blush.

**rub-er, -ra, -rum,** *adj.,* red.

**rub-or, -ōris,** 3 *m.,* blush.

**rūm-or, -ōris,** 3 *m.,* report, rumour.

**rump-o, -ere, rūpi, ruptum,** 3, break, burst.

**ru-o, -ere, -i, -tum,** 3, rush, fall headlong, come to ruin.

**rūp-ēs, -is,** 3 *f.,* rock, cliff.

**rursus** (*or* **rursum**), *adv.,* again.

**rūs, rūris,** 3 *n.,* country

**S**

**Sabīnus,** *adj.,* belonging to a district N.E. of Rome.

**Sacae,** 1 *m. pl.,* Sacians, a Scythian people.

**sacculus,** 2 *m.,* little bag, purse.

**sac-er, -ra, -rum,** *adj.,* sacred.

**saeclum** *or* **saeculum,** 2 *n.,* age, generation.

**saepe,** *adv.,* often.

**saep-io, -īre, -si, -tum,** 4, fence in.

**Saetabus,** *adj.,* of Saetabis, a town in Spain.

**saevus,** *adj.,* violent, savage.

**sagittifer, -a, -um,** *adj.,* arrow-bearing.

**sal, salis,** 3 *m.,* salt, sea, wit.

**salapūtium,** 2 *n.,* manikin.

**sal-io, -īre, -ui, -tum,** 4, leap, dance.

**Salisubsilus,** 2 *m.,* a name of Mars with reference to his dancing priests.

**salsus,** *adj.,* salt, witty.

**saltus,** 4 *m.,* glade, lawn.

**sal-ūs, -ūtis,** 3 *f.,* safety.

**salvē,** *interj.,* hail !

**sanctus,** *adj.,* sacred.

**sānē,** *adv.,* indeed.

**sangu-is, -inis,** 3 *m.,* blood.

**sap-io, -ere, -ii, —,** 3, be wise, know.

**satis,** *adv.,* enough.

**Sāturnāli-a, -ōrum,** 2 *n., pl.,* festival of the Saturnalia (Dec. 17th).

**saxeus,** *adj.,* of rock, stony.

**Scamand-er, -ri,** 2 *m.,* Scamander, a river near Troy.

**scelestus,** *adj.,* wicked, infamous.

**scel-us, -eris,** 3 *n.,* crime.

**scīlicet,** *adv.,* doubtless, you may be sure.

scio, 4, be skilled in, know.
scrīb-o, -ere, scripsi, scriptum, 3, write.
scrīnium, 2 n., book-case, desk.
scriptum, 2 n., writing, book.
scurra, 1 m., jester, dandy.
sē, sui, *reflex. pron.*, himself, herself, themselves.
sēcrētus, *adj.*, lonely, secret.
secto (*usually* sector, *dep.*), 1, pursue.
secundus, *adj.*, second, following, favourable.
secūr-is, -is, 3 *f.*, axe.
sed, *conj.*, but.
sed-eo, -ēre, sēdi, sessum, 2, sit.
semel, *adv.*, once.
sēmihian-s, -tis, *adj.* half-open.
sēmimortuus, *adj.*, half-dead.
semper, *adv.*, always, for ever.
seneo, 2, to be old.
sen-esco, -escere, -ui, —, 3, grow old.
sen-ex, -is, 3 *m.*, old man.
sensus, 4 *m.*, sense, feeling.
sen-tio, -tīre, -si, -sum, 4, feel, think, perceive.
sep-elio, -elīre, -elīvi, -ultum, 4, bury.
septemgeminus, *adj.*, sevenfold.
Septimillus, 2 *m.*, a pet name for Septimius.
Septimius, 2 *m.*, Septimius, a friend of Catullus.
sepulcrum, 2 *n.*, tomb.
sequ-or, -i, secūtus, sum, 3 *dep.*, follow.
Serāpis, -is, 3 *m.*, Serapis, an Egyptian god.
serm-o, -ōnis, 3 *m.*, talk, discussion.
servio, 4, be enslaved, serve.

Sestiānus, *adj.*, of Sestus.
Sestius, Sestius, a dull lawyer.
seu, *see* sīve.
sevērus, *adj.*, stern, strict.
sēvoco, 1, call apart, withdraw.
sī, *conj.*, if.
sībilus, 2 *m.*, a hissing, whistling ; also *adj.*
sīc, *adv.*, thus, so, to this extent.
sīcut, *adv.*, just as, like.
sīd-us, -eris, 3 *n.*, star.
signum, 2 *n.*, sign, standard.
silesc-o, -ere, —, —. 3, become silent.
silva, 1 *f.*, wood, forest.
silvestr-is, -e, *adj.*, wooded, living in woods.
simil-is, -e, *adj.*, like.
Simōnidēus, *adj.*, of Simonides, a Greek lyric poet.
simul, *adv.*, at the same time, at once.
sincērē, *adv.*, honestly.
sine, *prep. with abl.*, without.
singulus, *adj.*, one each, separate, single.
sinist-er, -ra, -rum, left, unfavourable.
sin-o, -ere, sīvi, situm, 3, permit.
sinus, 4 *m.*, bay, bosom.
sī-quis, -qua, -quid, *indef. pron.*, if anyone, anything.
Sirmi-o, -ōnis, 3 *m.*, Sirmio, a peninsula on Lake Garda.
sīve, seu, whether ; sive . . . sive, whether . . . or.
soccus, 2 *m.*, low-heeled shoe, slipper.
sodāl-is, -is, 3 *m.*, friend, companion.
sōl, sōlis, 3 *m.*, sun.
sōlāciolum, 2 *n.*, *dim.* of sōlācium, comfort.
sōlācium, 2 *n.*, consolation.

solea, 1 *f.*, sandal, slipper.
sol-eo, -ēre, **solitus sum,** 2 *semi-dep.*, be accustomed.
sōlor, 1 *dep.*, comfort, console.
sōlus, *adj.*, alone, solitary.
sol-vo, -vere, -vi, -ūtum, 3, loosen, pay.
somnus, 2 *m.*, sleep.
sonitus, 4 *m.*, sound, noise.
son-o, -āre, -ui, -itum, 1, sound, speak.
sop-or, -ōris, 3 *m.*, slumber.
sordidus, *adj.*, unclean, foul.
sor-or, -ōris, 3 *f.*, sister.
sospito, 1, save, preserve.
specto, 1, look at, behold.
specus, 4 *m.*, cave, grotto.
spern-o, -ere, sprēvi, sprē-tum, 3, scorn.
spēro, 1, hope.
splendidus, *adj.*, bright, shin-ing, brilliant.
sponsum, 2 *n.*, covenant, agree-ment.
stagnum, 2 *n.*, pool, lake.
stern-uo, -uere, -ui, —, 3, sneeze.
stīp-es, -itis, 3 *m.* tree-trunk, tree.
stirp-s, -is, 3 *f.*, trunk, root, stock, race.
sto, stāre, steti, statum, 1, stand.
stolidus, *adj.*, dull, obtuse.
strophium, 2 *n.*, breast-band.
stud-eo, -ēre, -ui, —, 2, be eager, apply oneself, desire, (*with dat.*).
studium, 2 *n.*, eagerness, desire.
stup-or, -ōris, 3 *m.*, dullness; amazement.
suāvior, 1 *dep.*, kiss.
suāv-is, -e, *adj.*, sweet, pleasant.
sub, *prep. with acc. or abl.* under, beneath.

subdū-co, -cere, -xi, -ctum, 3, remove, withdraw, reckon.
sub-eo, -īre, -ii, -itum, 4, come up, submit to.
subito, *adv.*, suddenly.
sublevo, 1, lift up, alleviate, console.
subsellium, 2 *n.*, bench.
sub-sterno, -sternere, -strāvi, -strātum, 3, strew under, spread beneath.
subter, *adv. and prep. with acc. and abl.*, below, underneath.
subtīl-is, -e, *adj.*, fine, delicate.
suburbānus, *adj.*, near the city.
suc-cumbo, -cumbere -cub-ui, -cubitum, 3, sink down, yield.
sūdārium, 2 *n.*, handkerchief, napkin.
suesc-o, -ere, suēvi, suētum, 3, become accustomed.
Suffēnus, 2 *m.*, Suffenus, a poetaster.
Sulla, 1 *m.*, Sulla, a gram-marian.
sum, esse, fui, to be.
sum-mitto, -mittere, -mīsi, -missum, 3, lower, yield.
summus, *adj.*, topmost, top of.
sumptuōsus, *adj.*, costly, sump-tuous.
suopte = suo (*emphatic suffix*).
super, *adv. and prep. with acc. and abl.*, over, beyond.
supero, 1, surpass.
supīnus, *adj.*, lying on the back, upturned.
suppernātus, *adj.*, lamed in the hip, cut down.
supplicium, 2 *n.*, punishment.
surg-o, -ere, **surrexi, surrec-tum,** 3, rise

**surrēp-o, -ere, -si, -tum, 3,** creep along.

**surrip-io, -ere, -ui, surreptum, 3,** filch, purloin, rob.

**sus-cipio, -cipere, -cēpi, -ceptum, 3,** take up, assume, suffer.

**suspicor, 1** *dep.*, suspect.

**suus,** *adj.*, his, her, its or their own.

**Syria, 1** *f.*, Syria, a province of Asia Minor.

### T

**tabella, 1** *f.*, tablet.

**tac-eo, 2,** be silent.

**taeda, 1** *f.*, pine tree, torch.

**taed-et, -ēre, -uit, —, 2** *impers.*, it wearies.

**taet-er, -ra, -rum,** *adj.*, repulsive, loathsome.

**talentum, 2** *n.*, talent (a Greek standard of money).

**tāl-is, -e,** *adj.*, such.

**tam,** *adv.*, so, to such a degree.

**tamen,** *conj.*, however.

**tandem,** *adv.*, at last.

**tang-o, -ere, tetigi, tactum, 3,** touch.

**tantum,** *adv.*, so much, so greatly, only.

**tantundem,** *adv.*, just so much.

**tantus,** *adj.*, so great.

**tardē,** *adv.*, slowly.

**tardo, 1,** hinder, delay.

**tardus,** *adj.*, slow, sluggish.

**taurus, 2** *m.*, bull.

**tectum, 2** *n.*, roof, dwelling.

**te-go, -gere, -xi, -ctum, 3,** cover, conceal, protect.

**Tēlemachus, 2** *m.*, son of Odysseus.

**tell-ūs, -ūris, 3** *f.*, earth, land.

**Tempē, 3** *n. pl.*, a valley in Thessaly.

**templum, 2** *n.*, temple.

**tempto, 1,** make trial of, try.

**temp-us, -oris, 3** *n.*, time; 29. 158, temples of the head.

**ten-ax, -ācis,** *adj.*, steadfast, obstinate.

**tenebrae, 1** *f. pl.*, shades, darkness.

**tenebricōsus,** *adj.*, dark, gloomy.

**tenellus, tenellulus,** *dim. adj.*, very delicate.

**ten-eo, -ēre, -ui, -tum, 2,** hold, grasp.

**tener, -a, -um,** *adj.*, tender.

**tenu-is, -e,** *adj.*, thin, meagre.

**tepe-facio, -facere, -fēci, -factum, 3,** make warm.

**tepidus,** *adj.*, lukewarm.

**tep-or, -ōris, 3** *m.*, warmth.

**tere-s, -tis,** *adj.*, smooth, polished.

**tergum, 2** *n.*, back.

**terra, 1** *f.*, earth.

**terr-or, -ōris, 3** *m.*, fear, alarm.

**tertius,** *adj.*, third.

**test-is, -is, 3** *c.*, witness.

**thalamus, 2** *m.*, bedroom, marriage chamber.

**Thēs-eūs, -ei** *and* **-eos,** *m.*, Theseus, famous Greek hero.

**Thespius,** *adj.*, of Thespiae, a town in Boeotia sacred to the Muses.

**Thessalus,** *adj.*, Thessalian.

**Theti-s, -idis, 3** *f.*, Thetis, mother of Achilles.

**thiasus, 2** *m.*, dance in honour of Bacchus.

**Thrācia, 1** *f.*, Thrace, a region of N. Greece.

**Thȳ-as, -adis, 3** *f.*, a Bacchante.

**Thȳnia, 1** *f.*, Bithynia.

**tībīc-ēn, -inis, 3** *m.*, fluteplayer.

**Tĭbur-s, -tis,** *adj.* of Tibur, a district N.E. of Rome.

**timeo,** 2, fear.

**tinnulus,** *adj.,* tinkling, shrill.

**tintino,** 1, jingle, ring.

**toll-o, -ere, sustuli, sublātum,** 3, lift up, carry off.

**torpeo,** 2, be inactive, falter.

**torp-or, -ōris,** 3 *m.,* numbness, inactivity.

**Torquātus,** 2 *m.,* a surname of the *gens Manlia.*

**torr-eo, -ēre, -ui, tostum,** 2, burn, scorch.

**torus,** 2 *m.,* couch.

**tot,** *adj. indec.,* so many.

**totidem,** *adj. indec.,* just as many.

**tōtus,** *adj.,* whole, entire.

**trab-s, -is,** 3 *f.,* beam, raft, ship.

**trā-do, -dere, -didi, -ditum,** 3, hand over, surrender.

**trans,** *prep. with acc.,* across, on the further side.

**trans-fero, -ferre, -tuli, -lātum,** bring over, translate.

**Transpadānus,** *adj.,* living beyond the river Po.

**trecenti,** *adj.,* three hundred.

**tremulus,** *adj.,* shaking, quivering, trembling.

**trepido,** 1, be agitated, tremble.

**tr-ēs, -ia,** *adj.,* three.

**tripudium,** 2 *n.,* a solemn dance.

**trist-is, -e,** *adj.,* sad, melancholy.

**Trīt-ōn, -ōnis,** 3 *m.,* a lake in Africa.

**trītus,** *see* tero.

**Trivia,** 1 *f.,* Diana, goddess of crossroads.

**Trivius,** *adj.,* of the crossroads.

**Trōia,** 1 *f.,* Troy.

**Trōicus,** *adj.,* Trojan.

**Trōjugena,** 1 *m.,* son of Troy, a Trojan.

**tru-x, -cis,** *adj.,* rough, fierce, savage.

**truncus,** *adj.,* maimed, mutilated.

**tū, tui,** *pron.,* thou, you.

**tu-eor, -ēri, tuitus sum,** 2 *dep.,* protect, guard, gaze upon.

**Tullius,** 2 *m.,* family name of Cicero.

**tum,** *adv.,* then.

**tunc,** *adv.,* then.

**tund-o, -ere, tutudi, tunsum** *or* **tūsum,** 3, beat, strike.

**turgidulus,** *adj.,* swollen.

**tuss-is, -is,** 3 *f.,* cough.

**tūtām-en, -inis,** 3 *n.,* protection, safeguard.

**tūtē,** *adv.,* safely, without danger.

**tūtus,** *adj.,* safe.

**tuus,** *adj.,* thy, your.

**tympanum,** 2 *n.,* drum.

**Tyrius,** *adj.,* of Tyre, Tyrian.

**U**

**ubi,** *adv.,* where, when.

**ubicumque,** *adv.,* wherever.

**ulcisc-or, -i, ultus sum,** 3 *dep.,* avenge oneself, punish.

**ullus,** *adj.,* any.

**ulmus,** 2 *f.,* elm.

**ulna,** 1 *f.,* elbow, arm.

**ultimus,** *adj.,* farthest, last.

**ultus,** *see* ulciscor.

**ululo,** 1, shriek, howl.

**Umb-er, -ra, -rum,** *adj.,* of Umbria, Umbrian ; *also subst.,* 2 *m.,* an Umbrian.

**umbilĭcus,** 2 *m.,* knob.

**umbra,** 1 *f.,* shade, shadow.

**ūm-or, -ōris,** 3 *m.,* fluid, moisture.

**umquam,** *adv.,* ever.
**ūnanimus,** *adj.,* of one mind, in accord.
**unctus,** *adj.,* anointed, rich.
**unda,** 1 *f.,* wave.
**unde,** *adv.,* whence.
**unguentum,** 2 *n.,* ointment.
**ungu-is, -is,** 3 *m.,* nail, claw.
**ūnicus,** *adj.,* only, sole.
**ūnus,** *adj.,* one, single.
**Ûrania,** 1 *f.,* a name of Venus.
**urbānus,** *adj.,* of the city, cultivated, elegant.
**urb-s, -is,** 3 *f.,* city.
**ur-geo, -gēre, -si, —,** 2, impel, press on.
**ūro, ūrere, ussi, ustum,** 3, burn.
**urtĭca,** 1 *f.,* nettle.
**usquam,** *adv.,* anywhere, in any way.
**usque,** *adv.,* continuously, as far as, as long as.
**usquequāque,** *adv.,* everywhere, on all occasions.
**ut,** *conj. with ind.,* as, when, where ; *with subj.,* in order that, so that.
**ut-er, -ra, -rum,** *interrog. adj.,* which of two?
**ut-erque, -raque, -rumque,** *pron. and adj.,* both, each of two.
**ūt-or, -i, ūsus sum,** 3 *dep.,* use (*with abl.*).
**utrum,** *conj.,* whether.
**ūva,** 1 *f.,* grape, vine.
**ux-or, -ōris,** 3 *f.,* wife.

### V

**vacuus,** *adj.,* empty.
**vād-o, -ere, —, —,** 3, go, rush.
**vadum,** 2 *n.,* shallow, ford.
**vae,** *interj.,* alas!
**vagor,** 1 *dep.,* wander.

**vagus,** *adj.,* wandering.
**val-eo,** 2, be well ; **valē,** farewell!
**vario,** 1, change, diversify.
**varius,** *adj.,* diverse, varying.
**Vārus,** 2 *m.,* Varus, a friend of Catullus.
**vasto,** 1, lay waste.
**vastus,** *adj.,* immense.
**Vatīniānus,** *adj.,* of Vatinius.
**Vatīnius,** 2 *m.,* an associate of Caesar, attacked by Catullus.
**-ve,** *encl. conj.,* or.
**vehemen-s, -tis,** *adj.,* violent, powerful.
**ve-ho, -here, -xi, -ctum,** 3, carry.
**vel,** *conj.,* or, even.
**vēlo,** 1, conceal, enwrap.
**velut,** *conj.,* just as, as if.
**venēnum,** 2 *n.,* poison.
**venia,** 1 *f.,* indulgence, forgiveness.
**ven-io, -īre, vēni, ventum,** 4, come.
**vent-er, -ris,** 3 *m.,* belly.
**ventito,** 1, come often.
**ventōsus,** *adj.,* windy, gusty.
**ventus,** 2 *m.,* wind.
**Ven-us, -eris,** 3 *f.,* Venus, goddess of love.
**venust-ās, -ātis,** 3 *f.,* charm, loveliness.
**venustus,** *adj.,* charming, graceful.
**Verāniolus,** 2 *m.,* a pet name for Veranius.
**Verānius,** 2 *m.,* Veranius, a friend of Catullus.
**vēr, vēris,** 3 *n.,* spring.
**verbum,** 2 *n.,* word.
**vērē,** *adv.,* really, in truth.
**ver-eor, -ēri, veritus sum,** 2 *dep.,* respect, fear.
**vēridicus,** *adj.,* truthful.

**Vērōna,** 1 *f.*, Catullus's native city.

**versiculus,** 2 *m.*, *dim. of* **versus,** verse.

**verso,** 1, turn, whirl, disturb.

**versus,** 4 *m.*, line of poetry, verse.

**vert-ex, -icis,** 3 *m.*, whirlpool, peak, head.

**vērum,** 2 *n.*, truth.

**vērum,** *adv. and conj.*, truly, but, however.

**vērus,** *adj.*, true.

**vēsānus,** *adj.*, mad.

**Vesper, -i** *or* **-is,** 2 *or* 3 *m.*, evening, evening star.

**vestibulum,** 2 *n.*, porch, entrance.

**vestīgium,** 2 *n.*, track, footstep.

**vest-is, -is,** 3 *f.*, robe, garment.

**veternus,** 2 *m.*, lethargy, sluggishness.

**vet-us, -eris,** *adj.*, old.

**via,** 1 *f.*, way, road.

**vic-em, -is,** (*no nom.*), 3 *f.*, change, misfortune, fate; *prep. with gen.*, instead of.

**victima,** 1 *f.*, victim for sacrifice.

**vict-or, -ōris,** 3 *m.*, conqueror.

**vidēn**=**videsne.**

**vid-eo, -ēre, vīdi, vīsum,** 2, see.

**viduus,** *adj.*, widowed.

**vig-esco, -escere, -ui, —,** 3, become lively or vigorous.

**vīl-is, -e,** *adj.* cheap, worthless.

**villa,** 1 *f.*, country house.

**villula,** 1 *f.*, *dim. of* **villa.**

**vin-cio, -cīre, -xi, -ctum,** 4, bind.

**vinculum,** 2 *n.*, bond, fetter.

**Vīnia,** 1 *f.*, Vinia, bride of Manlius.

**vīnum,** 2 *n.*, wine.

**violo,** 1, outrage.

**vir, -i,** 2 *m.*, man, husband.

**vireo,** 2, flourish, be vigorous, be green.

**virg-o, -inis,** 3 *f.*, maiden.

**virid-is, -e,** *adj.*, green.

**virt-ūs, -ūtis,** 3 *f.*, manliness, bravery, virtue.

**vīs,** 3 *f.*, violence ; *pl.* **vires,** strength.

**vī-so, -sere, -si, -sum,** 3, look at, visit.

**vīta,** 1 *f.*, life.

**vīt-is, -is,** 3 *f.*, vine.

**vīto,** 1, avoid, escape.

**vīv-o, -ere, vixi, victum,** 3, live.

**vīvus,** *adj.*, alive.

**vix,** *adv.*, scarcely.

**voco,** 1, call.

**volito,** 1, flit about, flutter.

**volo,** 1, fly.

**volo, velle, volui,** wish.

**volunt-ās, -ātis,** 3 *f.*, wish, inclination.

**volupt-ās, -ātis,** 3 *f.*, pleasure, desire.

**vorāg-o, -inis,** 3 *f.*, abyss, whirlpool, depth.

**voro,** 1, devour.

**vōtum,** 2 *n.*, promise, vow, prayer.

**vox, vōcis,** 3 *f.*, voice, sound.

**vulgus,** 2 *n.*, crowd, multitude.

## Z

**Zephyrus,** 2 *m.*, the west wind.

**zōna,** 1 *f.*, belt, girdle.

**zōnula,** 1 *f.*, *dim.* of **zōna,** girdle.

# GEORGE ALLEN & UNWIN LTD

*Head Office:*
*London: 40 Museum Street, W.C.1*

*Trade orders and enquiries:*
*Park Lane, Hemel Hempstead, Herts*

*Athens: 7 Stadiou Street, Athens 125*
*Auckland: P.O. Box 36013, Auckland 9*
*Barbados: Rockley New Road, St. Lawrence 4*
*Bombay: 103/5 Fort Street, Bombay 1*
*Calcutta: 285J Bepin Behari Ganguli Street, Calcutta 12*
*Dacca: Alico Building, 18 Motijheel, Dacca 2*
*Ibadan: P.O. Box 62*
*Johannesburg: P.O. Box 23134, Joubert Park*
*Karachi: Karachi Chambers, McLeod Road, Karachi 2*
*Lahore: 22 Falettis' Hotel, Egerton Road*
*Madras: 2/18 Mount Road, Madras 2*
*Manila: P.O. Box 157, Quezon City, D-502*
*Mexico: Serapio Rendon 125, Mexico 4, D.F.*
*Nairobi: P.O. Box 30583*
*New Delhi: 4/21-22B Asaf Ali Road, New Delhi 1*
*Ontario: 2330 Midland Avenue, Agincourt*
*Rio de Janeiro: Caixa Postal 2537-ZC-00*
*Singapore: 248C-6 Orchard Road, Singapore 9*
*Sydney, N.S.W. 2000: Bradbury House, 55 York Street*
*Tokyo: C.P.O. Box 1728, Tokyo 100-91*

# GILBERT MURRAY

## *The Translations of Greek Plays*

### AESCHYLUS

THE AGAMEMNON

THE CHOËPHOROE

THE EUMENIDES

THE SUPPLIANT WOMEN

PROMETHEUS BOUND

THE SEVEN AGAINST THEBES

THE PERSIANS

### EURIPIDES

ALCESTIS

ELECTRA

HIPPOLYTUS

IPHIGENIA IN TAURIS

MEDEA

RHESUS

THE TROJAN WOMEN

ION

BACCHAE

### SOPHOCLES

OEDIPUS, KING OF THEBES

THE ANTIGONE

THE WIFE OF HERACLES

OEDIPUS AT COLONUS

### ARISTOPHANES

THE FROGS

THE BIRDS

THE KNIGHTS

### MENANDER

THE ARBITRATION

THE RAPE OF THE LOCKS

*

## THE ORESTEIA
## THE COMPLETE PLAYS OF AESCHYLUS
## COLLECTED PLAYS OF EURIPIDES

GEORGE ALLEN AND UNWIN LTD